CHILTON'S Repair and Tune-Up Guide

Audi Fox

ILLUSTRATED

Prepared by the

Automotive Editorial Department

Chilton Book Company

Chilton Way
Radnor, Pa. 19089
215—687-8200

president and chief executive officer **WILLIAM A. BARBOUR;** executive vice president **K. ROBERT BRINK;** vice president and general manager **WILLIAM D. BYRNE;** editor-in-chief **JOHN D. KELLY;** managing editor **JOHN H. WEISE, S.A.E.;** assistant managing editor **PETER J. MEYER;** senior editor **STEPHEN J. DAVIS;** editor **JOHN G. MOHAN;** technical editors **Ronald L. Sessons, N. Banks Spence Jr**

CHILTON BOOK COMPANY   RADNOR, PENNSYLVANIA

Copyright © 1975 by Chilton Book Company
First Edition
All Rights Reserved
Published in Radnor, Pa. by Chilton Book Company
and simultaneously in Ontario, Canada
by Thomas Nelson & Sons, Ltd.
Manufactured in the United States of America

Library of Congress Cataloging in Publication Data

Chilton Book Company, Automotive Editorial Dept.
   Chilton's repair and tune-guide, Audi Fox.

   1. Audi Fox automobile. I. Title. II. Title:
Repair and tune-up guide, Audi Fox.
TL215.A8C48 1975   629.28'7'22   75-33268
ISBN 0-8019-6336-2
ISBN 0-8019-6337-0 pbk.

ACKNOWLEDGMENT

Chilton Book Company expresses appreciation to the following
for their generous assistance:

Algar Porsche Audi
1234 Lancaster Ave.
Rosemont, Pennsylvania 19010

Contents

iii

Chapter One

General Information and Maintenance

How To Use This Book

Chilton's Repair and Tune-Up Guide for the Audi Fox is intended to acquaint the Fox owner with the systems of his machine in order for him to keep it running properly and in the process, save money. The first two chapters are the most important, since they contain the most commonly used information and procedures. They are: "General Information and Maintenance", and "Tune-Up and Troubleshooting." With the simple steps contained in them, the average Fox owner can save himself the cost of the book in his first do-it-yourself repair.

The following eight chapters of the book are concerned with the major systems of the Fox. Along with the simplified steps, a variety of illustrations are supplied to help the reader better understand exactly what any given procedure entails. In this book, we will not go into areas that are beyond the scope of the average owner-mechanic. Where a special tool or process is needed, it will be pointed out.

Before attempting any job outlined in this book, read through the entire procedure, to make sure that you have it straight in your mind, and to make sure that you know exactly what tools and/or parts will be needed for that operation. There is nothing as frustrating and expensive as getting halfway into a job and realizing that there is no possible way that you can finish it.

At this point, two items basic to any discussion of automotive repair should be mentioned. First, whenever the left side of the car is mentioned, you should realize that this is the drivers side; and conversely, the right side is the passenger side. Second, most screws and bolts are removed by turning them counterclockwise, and tightening by turning clockwise. When removing bolts and screws that have been exposed to the weather, it is a good idea to apply some penetrating oil to the bolts and work them carefully back and forth as they are being removed. As little time spent here will lessen the chances of having to use an "easy-out" on a snapped off bolt.

When working on a car, remember that safety is the most important rule. Constantly be aware of the dangers of working on an automobile and take proper precautions. Use jackstands when working under a raised car; don't smoke or

1

allow an exposed flame near the battery or any part of the fuel system. Always use the proper tool, shortcutting when it comes to tools will cause you grief sooner or later.

Cleanliness, often overlooked by the "at home" type mechanic, can be just as important as having the proper equipment for a job. A tiny part lost amid the grime of a dirty engine compartment will cause a frustrating delay that could have been avoided if the work area was cleaned beforehand. Once you have some experience and gain confidence, working on your car will become both an enjoyable and money saving experience.

Tools and Equipment

The following list is a basic requirement to perform most of the procedures listed in this book. The Fox is assembled with metric screws and bolts; if you don't have a good set of metric wrenches, buy one. Standard wrenches do not fit properly on metric parts.

1. Metric sockets with a $^{13}/_{16}$ in. spark plug socket.

2. Set of metric combination wrenches. Combination wrenches have one open end, and one box end.

3. Wire type spark plug gauge.

4. A flat feeler gauge for checking the breaker points and valve lash. (0.016, 0.010, and 0.018 in. sizes)

5. Slot and phillips head screwdrivers.

6. Timing light, preferably a DC battery hookup type, i.e., one that receives its power supply directly from the battery.

7. Dwell-tachometer.

8. Valve adjusting tools (VW 10-208 and VW 10-209). You'll need these tools if you plan on adjusting your valves yourself. They may be ordered through your Audi dealer.

9. A torque wrench. There are many types of torque wrenches available, the best being those that click when the specified torque is obtained. The use of a torque wrench ensures the proper tightening of fasteners to avoid either stripping (too tight) or leaks (too loose).

10. Oil can filler spout. This inexpensive item will avoid the spilling of oil all over the engine.

11. Oil filter strap wrench. This will make it much easier to remove a tight filter, it should never be used to install a filter.

12. A pair of vise grip pliers. These provide a multitude of uses when working on your car.

13. Two strong jackstands, sufficient to support the weight of the Fox. Makeshift supports such as cinderblocks are not safe enough to work under.

History

The Audi Fox is the American version of the Audi 80, as it is known in Europe. Introduced in 1973, with its clean looks and single overhead cam—front wheel drive design, has become very popular. While the Fox shares some parts with the larger 100 series, it is a totally new design.

Its suspension consists of MacPherson struts in the front, along with a stabilizer bar. In the rear, the axle is attached to two suspension arms which are in turn attached to coil spring-shock struts. A Panhard rod (stabilizer) is also used in the rear. The engine is an inline, single overhead cam, water-cooled, four-cylinder unit which is angled 20° in the engine compartment. A carbureted 1471 cc was used in 1973–74, but to meet emissions standards for 1975 without a catalyst (in 49 states) a larger fuel injected engine is used. This fuel injected 1588 cc engine produces 81 horsepower while getting between 21 and 34 miles per gallon. Also new for 1975 is a Fox station wagon. A combination of sports car performance and station wagon load space, power the Fox wagon from 0 to 50 mph in 8.5 seconds while providing 53.7 cubic feet of luggage space.

WARRANTY

Porsche Audi, a division of Volkswagen of America, Inc., sells each of its new cars with a 12 month or 20,000 mile warranty from the date of purchase. Unlike some other warranties, this one is

1973 Fox side view

1973 Fox front view

1974 Fox side view

1974 Fox front view

1975 Fox side view

1975 Fox station wagon

transferrable if the car is sold within the time allotment of the coverage.

This warranty covers the complete car including the battery and tires, provided certain maintenance is performed by an authorized dealer. There is a separate warranty covering the emission control system components of the Fox.

Chassis serial number location

Serial Number Identification

VEHICLE IDENTIFICATION PLATE

The vehicle identification plate is riveted to the inner right fender. On the plate are the date of manufacture and the chassis number.

CHASSIS NUMBER

The chassis number is located on the driver's side windshield pillar and is visible through the windshield. The chassis number is also stamped on the firewall over the windshield washer reservoir. It also appears on the vehicle identification plate. The chassis number follows the words "Fahrgest-Nr" on this plate. It is usually a ten digit code broken up into three sections.

ENGINE NUMBER

The engine number is stamped on the left-side of the engine block between the fuel pump and the distributor. This number may be hard to spot because of the grime that builds up with normal mileage. A rag soaked in solvent should make the numbers legible.

TRANSMISSION NUMBER

The transmission serial number is located between the distributor and the windshield washer unit.

Fox identification number locations

Engine number location

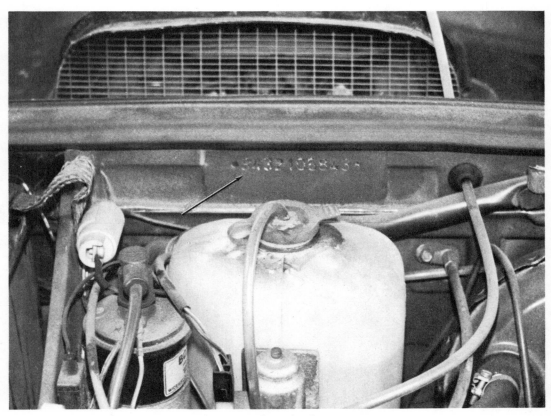

Chassis serial number location

Air cleaner element removal

Routine Maintenance

AIR CLEANER

You should remove and clean the air filter element every 10,000 miles and replace it every 20,000 miles or two years. The easiest way to clean an air filter is to blow it out from the inside out with compressed air being careful not to let the dust blow back into your eyes. Another less effective way, is to tap the element gently on the ground, being careful not to distort its shape.

The air cleaner's function is to prevent dust from entering the carburetor and then the engine. A clogged air filter will cause a decrease in performance and economy. The air filter is neither expensive nor difficult to replace, so there is no excuse why the engine should suffer the effects of a clogged air filter.

SERVICE

1973-EARLY 1975

1. Unsnap the 5 top cover retaining clips and remove the top.

2. Lift out the paper element. If it is very dirty, and you can not see the light of a flashlight shining through it, throw it away.

3. Wipe out the lower housing, clean-ing the temperature control valve (if applicable), and replace the element.

LATER 1975 MODELS

To remove the air filter undo the bottom clips and slide out the filter and housing from the bottom.

CRANKCASE VENTILATION

Blow-by gasses (they are gasses from the combustion process that by-passed the rings and entered the crankcase), are routed from the camshaft cover to the air cleaner for recirculation into the combustion process. The Fox system doesn't use a PCV (Positive Crankcase Ventilation) valve, like many other cars, but uses simple hoses instead. At every tune-up these hoses should be checked for clogging or deterioration, and cleaned and replaced as necessary. They should also be checked for looseness at every oil change, since engine vibration will have an effect on them. A clogged line will cause a build-up of crankcase pressure and result in oil leaks.

BELTS

Tension Checking, Adjusting, and Replacement

Push in on the drive belt about midway between the crankshaft pulley and the alternator. If the belt deflects more than $9/16$

Checking for proper belt deflection at point "a"

in. or less than ⅜ in., it's too loose or too tight. If the belt is frayed or cracked, replace it. Adjust belt tension as follows:

1. Loosen both nuts on the bracket.

2. When replacing the belt, pry the alternator toward the engine and slip the belt from the pulleys.

3. Carefully pry the alternator out with a bar, such as a ratchet handle or broom handle, and then tighten the alternator bracket nuts.

NOTE: *Be careful not to damage the alternator when pulling on it.*

4. Recheck the tension.

Since the alternator belt also drives the water pump, it is good insurance to carry a spare in your trunk. The key to belt tension, is remembering not to make the belts too tight or too loose; either condition is bad for the engine, a too loose belt will not drive the alternator properly, while a belt that's too tight will damage the water pump bearings.

NOTE: *The California air pump and the optional air conditioning belts are adjusted in the same manner. With more than one belt on the engine, it may be necessary to loosen the outer belts before the inner one can be adjusted.*

The air conditioner belt is adjusted by loosening the top four mounting bolts and sliding the unit toward the right fender to tighten and toward the left fender to loosen.

AIR CONDITIONING

This book contains no repair or maintenance procedures for the air conditioning

1. Compressor
2. Right condenser
3. Left condenser
4. Drier
5. Control valve
6. Evaporator
7. Temperature sensor
8. Air tunnel
9. Heater
10. Air vent

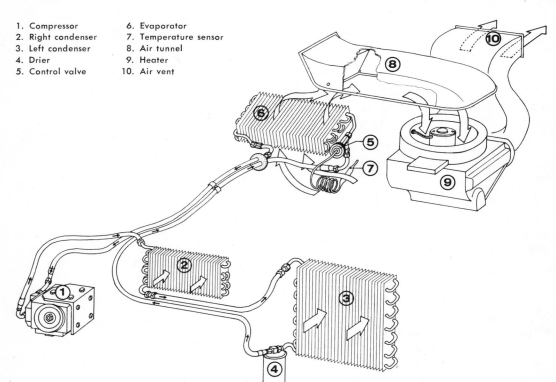

Air conditioning schematic; actual installation may be different from this picture.

system. It is recommended that any such repairs be left to the experts, who are are aware of the hazards and who have the proper equipment.

CAUTION: *The compressed refrigerant used in the air conditioning system expands into the atmosphere at a temperature of −21.7°F or lower. This will freeze any surface, including your eyes, that it contacts. In addition, the refrigerant decomposes into a poisonous gas in the presence of flame. Do not open or disconnect any part of the air conditioning system.*

Sight Glass Check

You can safely make a few simple checks to determine if your air conditioning system needs service. The tests work best if the temperature is warm (about 70°F).

1. Place the automatic transmission in Park or the manual transmission in Neutral. Set the parking brake.

2. Run the engine at a fast idle (about 1,500 rpm) either with the help of a friend, or by temporarily readjusting the idle speed screw.

3. Set the controls for maximum cold with the blower on high.

4. Locate the sight glass in one of the system lines. Usually it is on the left alongside the top of the radiator.

On the Fox it may be necessary to remove the top radiator trim panel in order to see the sight glass and clean the grille. To do this, see Chapter 3, "Engine and Engine Rebuilding."

5. If you see bubbles, the system must be recharged. Very likely there is a leak at some point.

6. If there are no bubbles, there is either no refrigerant at all or the system is fully charged. Feel the two hoses going to the belt driven compressor. If they are both at the same temperature, the system is empty and must be recharged.

7. If one hose (high pressure) is warm and the other (low pressure) is cold, the system may be alright. However, you are probably making these tests because you think there is something wrong, so proceed to the next step.

8. Have an assistant in the car turn the fan control on and off to operate the compressor clutch. Watch the sight glass.

9. If bubbles appear when the clutch is disengaged and disappear when it is engaged, the system is properly charged.

10. If the refrigerant takes more than 45 seconds to bubble when the clutch is disengaged, the system is overcharged. This usually causes poor cooling at low speeds.

Care

Many people who add air conditioning to a car know little about how to care for it. With just a few simple rules, this expensive option can easily be made to last the life of the car with no major repairs necessary.

1. Keep the condenser grille clean. Driving tends to build up debris on the grille which will cut down on the effective cooling that it can do for the system. It's also a good idea to check the radiator grille for debris, since an added strain is placed on it with the air conditioning unit.

2. Make sure that year round your cooling system has at least a 50/50 water to antifreeze mixture. Without a coolant added, the strain of the air conditioner unit will overheat the engine and may cause serious damage.

3. Every two years the system should be drained and flushed. Contaminants build up in the cooling system over a period of time, and in order to keep the system running at peak efficiency, it is necessary to periodically clean the system.

4. With the engine cool, inspect the radiator cap gaskets condition. A worn gasket will not seal the system effectively and as a result the performance of the air conditioner will decline.

5. Checking the drive belts, especially in the summer is very important. Replacing a belt that is about to fail will cause less inconvenience than having one snap when you're miles from a garage.

6. Check the condition of all the air conditioner hoses. Here again preventative maintenance will pay off in trouble free driving.

7. In the wintertime, when the last thing on your mind is air conditioning, turn on the air conditioner and run it for a few minutes. Doing this will keep it lubricated internally and add to its lifespan.

CAUTION: *If you determine that the system has a leak, take it to a qualified service center as soon as possible. A leak that is left to deteriorate will only create a larger repair bill when it is finally corrected.*

FLUID LEVEL CHECKS

Engine Oil

The oil level should be checked weekly as a matter of course; if you can't find time to do it yourself, then have it checked each time you get gas. Engine oil level should be checked with the car on level ground after the engine has been turned off for a few minutes. This allows the oil in the engine to drip back into the pan so an accurate reading can be obtained. The dipstick, which looks like a long thin rod with a curved handle, is located on the driver's side of the engine in front of the fuel pump.

1. Remove the dipstick and wipe it clean.
2. Reinsert it
3. Remove the dipstick. The oil level should be between the two marks. The difference between the two marks is one quart. The oil level should always be kept between the two marks.

Transaxle

MANUAL

The transaxle is the unit at the front of the car which supplies the force generated by the engine, to the front wheels. It is a combination transmission and differential. The oil level of the transaxle is checked at the filler plug opening located on the driver's side of the transaxle, behind the axle shaft. With a drain plug wrench, remove the plug and insert your

Transaxle drain plug (A) and filler plug (B) locations

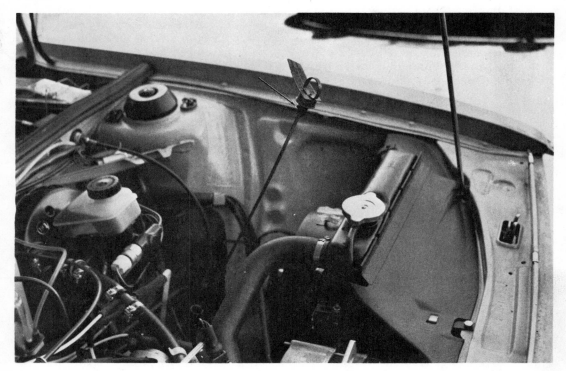

Automatic transaxle dipstick

finger. The oil level should be even with the level of the plug opening, if fluid leaks out when you unscrew the plug, the level is alright and the plug does not have to be removed. Top up if necessary with an SAE 80 or 90 gear oil. Use a pump type oil can, or hand bulb syringe to add fluid.

AUTOMATIC

The automatic transaxle dipstick is located at the left rear of the engine. Use the following procedure when checking the fluid level:

1. Idle the engine for a few minutes with the selector in Neutral. Apply the parking brake.

2. Remove the dipstick, wipe it clean, reinsert it, and withdraw it again.

3. The fluid level should be between the two marks. Add Dexron® or Type A transmission fluid. The difference between the two marks on the dipstick is less than one pint, so don't add ATF too quickly; too much ATF is as bad as too little. Use a long necked funnel to add fluid. Be careful not to spill automatic transmission fluid over a hot engine, as it can be dangerous.

Automatic Transaxle Final Drive

The final drive uses SAE 80 or 90 gear oil. The filler plug is located on the left-side of the unit directly behind the axle driveshaft. Check and add oil in the same manner as the manual transaxle.

Automatic transaxle lower unit filler plug

Brake Master Cylinder

The master cylinder is located on the left-side of the engine compartment at

Master cylinder level marks

the firewall. On top of it is a clear plastic container, the brake reservoir, with the words, "MIN" and "MAX" on it. Brake fluid level should be maintained at the "MAX" line on the reservoir. Each time you stop for gas the brake fluid level can be checked visually. If necessary, add enough brake fluid to bring the level up to the "MAX" level. The fluid that is to be used will be marked DOT 3 or 4 somewhere on the can.

Coolant

Make it a habit to periodically check the coolant level in the radiator. Ideally, this should be performed when the engine is cold. When checking the coolant level on a warm or hot engine, turn the cap to the first catch to permit pressure to be released from the system. Turn the cap off counterclockwise. A gauge plate inside the radiator aids in level checking—the coolant should be maintained at the bottom of the plate. Use only a quality ethylene glycol antifreeze to refill or top up the cooling system.

The cooling system should be drained, cleaned, and refilled every two years or 24,000 miles. There is a petcock or drain plug at the bottom of the radiator and a drain plug on the engine block to facilitate draining. Use one of the many commercially available cleaners to flush out the system. These remove rust and scale which cut down on cooling efficiency. Refill with the correct water/antifreeze solution for anticipated temperatures. An antifreeze percentage chart is included in the "Appendix."

Radiator drain plug location

1975 Foxes do not have a drain plug or petcock at the bottom of the radiator. To drain the coolant, you must disconnect the bottom radiator hose.

CAUTION: *Do this only when the engine is cold to avoid getting burned by the hot coolant.*

Steering Gear

The Audi Fox is equipped with rack and pinion steering which is filled at the factory with lubricant. There is no way to add additional grease to the system short of dismantling it, for this reason if you notice any peculiar leaking around the steering mechanism, have it checked at the dealer.

Battery

The battery on all 1973–74 Foxes is located at the rear of the engine compartment, at the firewall. On some 1975 models, the battery is located on the left side of the trunk. Fluid level in the battery should be checked frequently, especially in the summer when the heat will rapidly evaporate the battery fluid. The battery should not be neglected in the winter either, as it takes more electrical energy to turn over a cold engine.

The Fox battery on all 1973–74 models is located on the right-side of the engine compartment, near the firewall

On Foxes with the battery located in the trunk, the fuel pump ground wire is connected directly to the battery. If it becomes dislodged, the car will not start. Make sure that it is reconnected properly if the battery has to be disturbed for any reason.

Battery Care

A few minutes occasionally spent monitoring battery condition is worth saving hours of frustration when your car won't start due to a dead battery. Only distilled water should be used to top up the battery, as tap water, in many areas, contains harmful minerals. Two tools which will facilitate battery maintenance are a hydrometer and a squeeze bulb filler. These are cheap and widely available at automotive parts stores, hardware stores, etc. The specific gravity of the electrolyte should be between 1.27 and 1.20. Keep the top of the battery clean, as a film of dirt can sometimes completely discharge a battery. A solution of baking soda and water may be used to clean the top surface, but be careful to flush this off with clear water and that none of the solution enters the filler holes. Clean the battery posts and clamps with a wire brush to

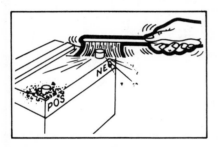

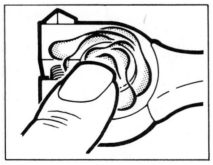

Smearing the battery terminals with petroleum jelly

eliminate corrosion deposits. Special clamp and terminal cleaning brushes are available for just this purpose. Lightly coat the posts and clamps with petroleum jelly or chassis grease after cleaning them.

TIRES AND WHEELS

One of the best, and the least expensive investments you can make for your Fox, is the addition of a tire pressure gauge. Service station gauges are generally either not working or inaccurate and should not be relied upon. There is a sticker on the back of the glove compartment lid that will tell you exactly what the tire pressure for your car should be. If you are using tires of a different type than the ones which the car was originally equipped, follow the manufacturer's instructions concerning inflation. Tires should be checked when they are cold, because air pressure increases with heat, and the readings will generally be 4–6 lbs higher after the tire has been run. For continued turnpike driving, or any continuous high speed driving, increase the tire pressure a few pounds all around. Never mix different kinds or sizes of tires on your Fox; different size tires will affect tire wear, and mixing radial and non-radials can result in unpredictable handling.

When removing the hub caps, make sure that the cap clips are properly positioned. If they are loose the cap will fall off. You can check for looseness by rotating the hub cap. If you can turn it, one or more of the clips are loose.

Tire Rotation

To obtain the maximum mileage from your tires, it is necessary to rotate them,

Capacities

| Year | Model | Engine Displacement Cu in. (cc) | Engine Crankcase (qts) | | Transmission (pts) | | Gasoline Tank (gals) | Cooling System (pts) |
			With Filter	Without Filter	Manual	Automatic		
1973–75	Fox	89.7 (1,471) 97.0 (1,588)	3.7	3.2	3.4①	6.4②	12.0③	13.0

① At change, initial amount 4.2 pts
② At change, initial amount 12.6 pts. Final drive contains 2.1 pts gear oil.
③ Not including 1.3 gal reserve

TIRE WEAR PATTERNS

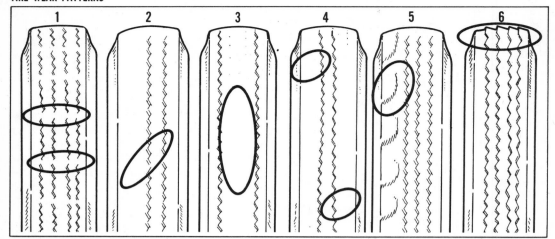

1. Tread Wear Bars. These appear when your tires are ready for replacement due to normal wear. The indicators are molded into the bottoms of the tread grooves. When bands appear in two or more adjacent grooves, replace the tire.
2. Incorrect Camber. When one side of the tire wears more rapidly than the other, suspect incorrect camber. If that side is worn smoothly, it means that a front end alignment is needed. Take the car to a specialist.
3. Overinflation. If your tires look as if only the center treads are wearing, you have been overinflating them. Find the proper inflation pressure in the Tire Inflation Chart. Check the tires with gauge of known accuracy and adjust pressure as necessary.
4. Underinflation. If the outer edges of your tires are wearing more than the center treads, you probably have them underinflated. Inflate the tires to the correct pressure as shown in the chart. Consider purchasing a tire pressure gauge which you can use to maintain correct pressure.
5. Cupping. This wear pattern can be caused by a number of problems. Misalignment resulting from bent steering linkage can cause this condition. A wheel/tire assembly that is out of balance can also cause this wear pattern.
6. Feathering. Saw-toothed wear patterns are caused by incorrect toe-in. Your front wheels must be turned inward slightly at the front. If this "toe-in" is excessive, however, the tires will wear in the pattern shown above. Have the front end alignment checked.

to equalize the wear, since in different positions on the car, tires wear differently. Tires should be rotated every 5–6,000 miles, according to the pattern shown on the illustration.

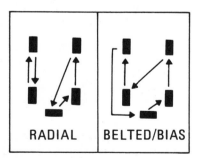

RADIAL   BELTED/BIAS

Use the radial tire pattern for rotating tires unless you are using bias-ply tires

Tire Pressure Chart

| Year | Model | Tire Size | Pressure (psi) | |
			Front	Rear
1973–75	All Sedans	155 x 13	28 (28)	30 (24)
1975	Wagon	All	28 (28)	34 (28)

Figure in parenthesis is for a light load

FUEL FILTER

The fuel filter is a strainer screen located under the top cover of the fuel pump. On the 1973–74 models, it should be replaced every 12,000 miles; on the 1975 Foxes, it should be replaced every 15,000 miles.

1. Disconnect the fuel line from the top cover of the pump.
2. Remove the single screw which retains the cover.
3. Lift off the cover and remove the strainer.
4. Clean the strainer in solvent and air dry.

Fuel pump strainer screen

Inline fuel filter (arrow)

5. Replace the strainer in the reverse order of removal.

In addition to the fuel pump strainer screen, all Foxes are also equipped with an inline type fuel filter. For 1973–74 this is located on the left-side of the engine near the fuel pump. It can be easily be found by tracing the fuel line from the fuel pump to the carburetor. The fuel pump is on the lower left of the engine block, the carburetor is on the upper right.

1975 Foxes with fuel injection use a similar type fuel filter, but this is located on the underside of the car, on the right-side by the fuel tank. This type is a fairly large silver container attached near the fuel tank.

To remove either type, the clips, nuts, or hose clamps must be removed and the fuel lines taken off the filter.

The 1973–74 filter can be reached by opening the hood and removing the connections from the top of the engine. The 1975 type filter must be removed from below the car; make sure that you plug the line from the tank so that the gas will not spill out.

Automatic Transaxle

The differential section of the automatic transaxle requires no attention

Automatic transaxle drain and filler plug locations

b. Automatic transaxle fluid drain plug
c. Automatic transaxle final drive (differential) drain plug
d. Automatic transaxle final drive filler plug
x. Automatic transaxle pan mounting bolts

other than a level check every 12 months or 12,000 miles. Top up with SAE 80 weight hypoid gear oil if you have a manual transaxle, and SAE 90 weight hypoid gear oil if you have an automatic transaxle.

Audi recommends that the automatic transaxle fluid be replaced every 30,000 miles (20,000 miles if your Fox is used for towing, mountain driving, or any other severe driving condition).

Changing the ATF

1. Buy 4 quarts of automatic transmission fluid, Dexron® with the letter B in front of the five digit code on the can.

2. Slide a drain pan under the trans-axle. Jack up the front of the car and support it safely on stands.

3. Remove the drain plug and allow all the fluid to drain.

4. Remove the pan retaining bolts and drop the pan.

5. Discard the old gasket and clean the pan with solvent.

6. Unscrew and clean the circular oil strainer.

7. Install the oil strainer, but don't tighten the bolt too much as the specified torque is only 2.5 ft lbs. Use a new gasket and install the pan.

8. Using a long-necked funnel, refill the transaxle with about 2¾ qts of fluid. Check the level with the dipstick. Run the car for a few minutes and check again.

Lubrication

OIL AND FUEL RECOMMENDATIONS

Your Fox is designed to operate on regular, low lead, or lead-free fuel, except in California. 1975 Foxes equipped with a catalytic converter must use lead-free fuel. The octane ratings are listed on the fuel cap door but these only have to be checked if you are travelling outside the U.S. If you are travelling in another country and are unsure about the octane rating of their regular, it would be a good idea to mix in some premium to raise the octane level a bit (except on 1975 models). Running your Fox on premium all the time though, will have no beneficial effect on the engine and will ruin the catalyst on 1975 models.

Oil must be selected with regard to the anticipated temperatures during the period before the next oil change. Using the chart, select the oil viscosity for the lowest expected temperature and you will be assured of easy cold starting and sufficient engine protection. The oil you pour into your Fox engine should have the designation "SE" marked on the top of its container. Under the classification system adopted by the American Petroleum Institute (API) in May, 1970, "SE" is the highest designation for passenger car use. The 'S' stands for passenger car use, and the second letter denotes a more specific application. "SA" oil, for instance, contains no additives and is suitable only for very light-duty usage. Oil designated "MS" (motor severe) may also be used, since this was the highest classification under the old API rating system.

Oil Viscosity Chart

Temperature Range	Recommended Viscosity
Below — 4° F	SAE 5W
	SAE 5W-20
— 4° to 32° F	SAE 10W
	10W-20 °
	10W-30 °
	10W-40 °
	10W-50 °
32° to 86° F	SAE 20W
	20W-50
Above 86° F	SAE 30W

° Denotes an oil that may be used year round

OIL CHANGES

Engine

Audi recommends you change your oil every 5,000 miles or three months for all Foxes through 1974. For all 1975 models, the interval is 7,500 miles. This interval is intended only for average driving, if your Fox is being used under severe circumstances, change the oil and filter sooner. Constant city driving is bad for your oil, and if you do much of it, you should change your oil more frequently so that the harmful acids and contaminants will not build up in your engine.

Always drain the oil after the engine has been run long enough to bring it to the normal operating temperature. Hot oil will flow easier and more contaminants will be removed with the oil than if it were drained cold. A large capacity drain pan, which can be purchased at any automotive supply store, will be more than paid back by savings from do-it-yourself oil changes. Another necessity is containers for the used oil, you will find that plastic bleach containers make excellent storage bottles.

The easiest way to dispose of old oil, is to cap the container that it is in and put it in the trash. Another solution would be to take it to a service station and ask them to dump it in their sump tank. Some of the old oil can be used over a protective coating for items that will be stored outdoors for a long period of time. A thin coat of oil on them will retard most forms of rust.

Oil Changing

1. Run the engine for a few minutes until it reaches its normal operating temperature.
2. Slide a drain pan under the oil pan drain plug. When reaching under, be careful not to touch anything hot.

3. Loosen the drain plug with a socket or box wrench, then remove it by hand. As the plug loosens, use one finger on each hand to turn it, so the hot oil doesn't spill all over your hand.
4. Allow all the oil to drain into the pan.
5. Replace the drain plug, making sure that the brass gasket is still attached to the plug. Tighten the plug to 18 ft lbs.

Manual Transaxle

It is relatively easy to change your own gear oil. The oil level should be checked twice a year and changed every 30,000 miles or three years, whichever comes first. The only equipment required is a drain pan, a wrench to fit the filler and drain plugs, and an oil suction gun. Gear oil can be purchased in gallon cans at the larger automotive supply stores.

To change the oil:
1. Jack up the front of the car and support it safely on stands.
2. Slide a drain pan under the transaxle.

Transaxle drain plug (A) and filler plug (B) locations

3. Remove the filler plug and then the drain plug.
4. When the oil has been completely drained, install the drain plug. Tighten to 18 ft lbs.
5. Using the suction gun, refill the gearbox or rear axle up to the level of the filler plug. Use an SAE 80 or 90 gear oil.
6. Install and tighten the filler plug.

OIL FILTER CHANGES

Audi recommends changing the oil at every other oil change, but it is better for the engine if the filter is changed at every oil change. The added expense will be worth it in the long run.

Changing the Filter

1. Drain the crankcase as stated above. Then move the drain pan under the filter.
2. The filter is on the left side of the engine, below the distributor. Reach in from the top and turn the filter counterclockwise to take it off. If it's too tight

Removing the oil filter

to remove by hand, use a strap wrench to loosen it.

3. Remove the filter and dispose of it somewhere where it won't hurt the environment. Wrapped in old newspapers and placed in the trash is a good solution, just make sure that none of the old oil drips on to the ground where it might cause some damage.

4. Clean the oil filter adapter (the place where the oil filter joins the engine) with a clean rag.

5. Lightly oil the rubber gasket on the new filter and spin it on the engine. Tighten it until the gasket connects with the engine, and then tighten it ½ to 1 turn more.

6. Start the engine and check for leaks.

CHASSIS GREASING

The Fox requires no chassis greasing and is not equipped with grease nipples. Check the axle driveshaft and tie rod rubber boots occasionally for leaking or cracking. At the same time, squirt a few drops of oil on the parking brake equalizer (point where cables V-off to the rear brakes). The front wheel bearings do not require greasing unless they are disassembled.

GENERAL LUBRICATION

Periodic lubrication will prevent squeaky, hard-to-open doors and lids. About every three months, pry the plastic caps off the door hinges and squirt in enough oil to fill the chambers. Press the plug back into the hinges after filling. Lightly oil the door check pivots. Finally, spray graphite lock lubricant on to your key and insert it into the door a few times.

The hood and trunk locks should be lubricated by an occasional few drops of oil. Two other areas that should be lubricated are the clutch cable connection next to the oil filter, and the parking brake compensating lever. Both of these should also get a few drops of oil now and ·then.

Jacking

The Audi Fox is equipped with a single rail, crank handle jack which fits the jack openings behind the front wheel and in front of the rear wheel. The car should never be jacked up by the bumper as this will damage the car. Never use the jack that came with the car for anything other than changing a flat tire: If you intend to use this book to do your own maintenance, a small hydraulic jack, a pair of jackstands, or drive-on ramps would be a good investment. Always chock the wheels when working on a car supported by a jack; it's surprising how little force it takes to move a car supported this way. If the wheels are not sufficiently blocked from moving, the force necessary to remove one stubborn lug nut, could bring the car down, causing a good deal of damage and/or injury.

Another point that has to be emphasized: NEVER WORK UNDER A CAR THAT IS SUPPORTED BY A JACK ALONE. This is asking for trouble. On the Fox, a jack can be safely placed under the front and rear jacking points, the engine crossmember (the heavy bar underneath the engine running from side to side), or the center of the rear axle beam. Make sure that the jack pad is at least 4 in. square when jacking the rear axle, or you may damage it. This expanded pad area is to more evenly distribute the jack load.

When jacking or hoisting the 1975 Foxes, be careful not to damage the fuel lines, especially those in the back of the car.

Pushing, Towing, and Jump Starting

If your Fox is equipped with a manual transaxle, it may be push started in an emergency. It should be recognized that there is the possibility of damaging bumpers and/or fenders of both cars. Make sure that the bumpers of both cars are evenly matched. Depress the clutch pedal, select Second or Third gear, and switch the ignition On. When the car reaches a speed of approximately 10 or 15 mph, release the clutch to start the engine. DO NOT ATTEMPT TO PUSH START AN AUTOMATIC FOX.

Fox front towing eye

Fox rear towing eye

Both manual and automatic Foxes may be towed short distances. Attach tow lines to the towing eye on the front suspension or the left or right bumper bracket at the rear. Automatic equipped cars must be towed no farther than 30 miles and no faster than 30 mph, unless the front wheels are off the ground.

If you plan on towing a trailer, don't exceed 992 lbs (trailer without brakes) or 1874 lbs (trailer with brakes. The trailer tongue load should be approximately 110 lbs. Towing a trailer with an automatic equipped Fox places an extra load on the transmission and a few items should be made of note here. Make doubly sure that the transmission fluid is at the correct level. Change the fluid more frequently if you're doing much trailer hauling. Start out in 1 or 2 and use the lower ranges when climbing hills. Aftermarket transmission coolers are available which greatly ease the load on your automatic and one should be considered if you often pull a trailer.

Jump starting is the favored method of starting a car with a dead battery. Make sure that the cables are properly connected, negative-to-negative and positive-to-positive, or you stand a chance of damaging the electrical systems of both cars. Keep the engine running in the donor car. If the car still fails to start, call a garage—continual grinding on the starter will overheat the unit and make repair or replacement necessary.

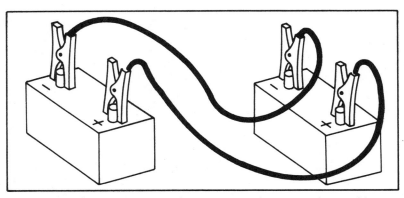

Proper connections for jump starting the Fox—negative-to-negative, positive-to-positive

Chapter Two

Tune-Up and Troubleshooting

Tune-Up Procedures

The procedures that follow will show you exactly how to tune your Fox in the simplest manner possible. A tune-up is essential for good gas mileage as well as maintaining the performance of your car. Audi recommends a complete tune-up every 9,000 miles for their 1973–74 Foxes, and every 15,000 miles for the 1975s. There is no mystery or tremendously complicated problem involved with doing a tune-up; it merely involves replacing parts that tend to wear with time. The three most commonly mentioned parts are: points, plugs, and condenser; these work together to ignite the fuel and air mixture inside the engine. The rotor and spark plug wires should also be replaced at this time if their condition warrants it.

It was, in the past, that a tune-up just concerned itself with the items mentioned above but as cars became more complicated with the addition of emissions control devices, these also had to be checked to ensure a proper tune-up. Procedures for checking these systems will be found in Chapter 4, "Emission Controls, and Fuel System." If you're experiencing some specific problem, turn to the "Troubleshooting" section at the rear of this chapter and follow the programmed format until you pinpoint the trouble. If you're just doing a tune-up to restore your Fox's pep and economy, proceed with the following steps.

It might be noted that a tune-up is a good time to look around the engine compartment for problems that might be just beginning, and take care of them before they can become major headaches. Look for oil and fuel leaks, deteriorating radiator and heater hoses, loose or fraying fan belts, and loose nuts or bolts. Also, since the automatic choke on the Fox is one that operates by water temperature, it is a good idea to check the hose connections going into the choke housing for looseness and/or wear.

SPARK PLUGS

Their primary job of igniting the air/fuel mixture aside, the spark plugs in your Fox can also serve as very useful diagnostic tools. Once removed, compare your spark plugs with the samples illustrated in section 4.6 of the "Troubleshooting" section at the end of this chapter. Typical plug conditions are shown along with their causes and remedies. Plugs which exhibit only normal wear and deposits can be cleaned, regapped, and installed. However it is a good prac-

Tune-Up Specifications

Year	Engine Displacement Cu in. (cc)	Spark Plugs * Type	Gap (in.)	Distributor Point Dwell (deg)	Point Gap (in.)	Ignition Timing (deg)	Intake Valve Opens (deg)	Compression Pressure (psi)	Idle Speed (rpm)	Valve Clearance (in.) In	Ex
1973	89 (1,471)	N8Y①	0.028	47–53	0.016	0 @ idle⑤	4B	8.2 : 1	850–1000	0.008–0.012	0.016–0.020
1974	89.7 (1,471)	N8Y②	0.028	47–53③	0.016	3A @ idle	4B	8.2 : 1	950	0.008–0.012	0.016–0.020
1975	97 (1,588)	N8Y④	0.028	47–53	0.016	3A @ idle	4B	8.0 : 1	900–950	0.008–0.012	0.016–0.020

* Champion brand plug listed, others footnoted
① Bosch plug—W175T30; Beru plug—175/14/3A
② Bosch plug—W175T30; Beru plug—175/14/3A
③ 47–53 in Calif.; 44–50 otherwise
④ Bosch plug—W215T2; Beru plug—215/14/3A
⑤ 30B @ 3,000 with vacuum hose disconnected
B Before top dead center
A After top dead center

tice to replace them at every major tune-up.

When replacing the plugs, it's a good idea to check the condition of the plug wires. If they're brittle or cracked, replace them, as they won't be able to do the job. A worn wire will not carry the full spark to the plug, and should it get wet, the wire will short out causing the engine to stall.

The Fox tool kit includes a spark plug socket and handle, but you will find it much more convenient to purchase a ½ in. drive, $^{13}/_{16}$ in. spark plug socket which can be turned with a ratchet handle. Using a small extension, all four plugs can be removed very quickly. Before removing the spark plug leads, number the towers on the distributor cap with tape. When applying the tape, first make sure that the surface it is going on is free of dirt and grease so the tape will stick properly. The firing order is 1-3-4-2, with the No. 1 cylinder at the front of the engine. This prevents mixups in the case of distributor cap replacement or spark plug wire replacement.

Removal and Installation

1. Grasp the No. 1 spark plug boot and pull straight out. Do not pull on the wire.

Removing loose dirt from around the plug prior to removal

Check the condition of the wire and the boot. If cracked, or worn, replace them. Proceed to the other plugs and repeat the operation. When you're finished, take a brush and remove any loose dirt from around the plug so that when it's removed no damaging grime will enter the engine.

2. Place the spark plug socket squarely on the plug. With a steady even pressure, turn the spark plug out of the cylinder head in a counterclockwise direction.

NOTE: *The Fox cylinder head is made of aluminum which is easily stripped. Remove the plugs only when the engine is cold.*

3. If removal is difficult, loosen the plug only sightly and drip some penetrating oil into the threads. Allow the oil enough time to work, and then unscrew

Number one spark plug with boot and protective cover removed

the plug. This way will ensure that you don't strip the threads when removing the plugs. If the plug is still difficult to remove with the penetrating oil on it work the plug back and forth as you remove it, but be careful not to break the ceramic insulator on the plug.

4. Repeat the operation with Nos. 2, 3, and 4 plugs.

5. Inspect the plugs using the "Troubleshooting" section illustrations that follow this chapter, and clean or discard them according to their condition. The plugs from your engine may not look exactly like the ones shown at the back of this chapter, those are just guides and not meant to look exactly like a plug from your engine, i.e., if your plug has oil on it, the oil fouling of your plug may be lighter or heavier than the one in the illustration.

New spark plugs come pre-gapped, but double check the setting or reset them if

Installing the spark plug hand-tight

Tightening the spark plug to the proper torque

you desire a different gap. The recommended spark plug gap is listed in the "Tune-Up Specifications" chart. Use a spark plug wire gauge for checking the gap. The wire should pass through the electrode with just a slight drag. Using the electrode bending tool on the end of the gauge, bend the side electrode to adjust the gap. Never attempt to adjust the center electrode. Lightly oil the threads of the replacement plug and install it hand-tight. It is a good practice to use a torque wrench to tighten the spark plugs on any car and especially on the Fox since the head is aluminum. Torque the spark plugs to 14–22 ft lbs. Install the ignition wire boots firmly on the spark plugs.

DWELL ANGLE

The dwell angle or cam angle is the number of degrees that the distributor cam rotates while the points are closed. There is an inverse relationship between dwell angle and point gap. Increasing the point gap will decrease the dwell angle. Checking the dwell angle with a meter is a far more accurate method of measuring point opening than the feeler gauge method.

After setting the point gap to specification with a feeler gauge as described above, check the dwell angle with a meter. Attach the dwell meter according to the manufacturer's instruction sheet. A typical dwell meter hook-up is illustrated in the "Tune-Up" section at the end of the chapter. The negative lead is grounded and the positive lead is connected to the primary wire terminal No. 1 that runs from the coil to the distributor. Start the engine, let it idle and reach operating temperature, and observe the dwell on the meter. The reading should fall within the allowable range. If it does not, the gap will have to be reset or the breaker points will have to be replaced.

BREAKER POINTS AND CONDENSER

Snap off the two retaining clips on the distributor cap. Remove the cap and examine it for cracks, deterioration, or carbon tracking. Replace the cap, if necessary, by transferring one wire at a time from the old cap to the new one. Examine the rotor for corrosion or wear and re-

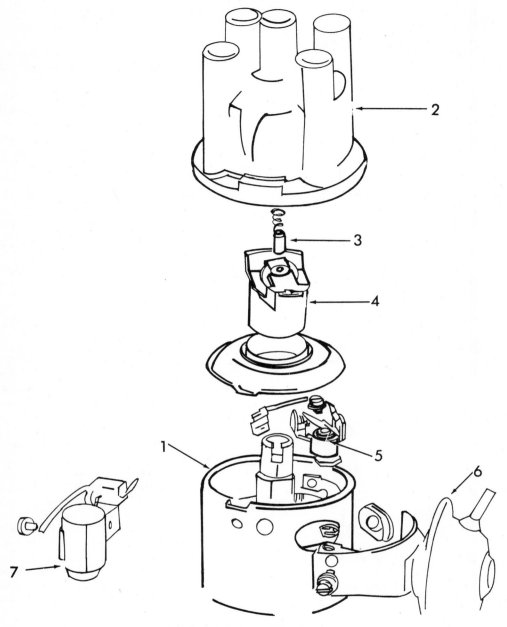

Exploded view of distributor

1. Distributor
2. Distributor cap
3. Carbon brush and spring
4. Rotor
5. Contact points
6. Vacuum advance unit
7. Condenser

place it if it's at all questionable. Remove the dust shield by pulling it off. Check the points for pitting and burning. Slight imperfections on the contact surface may be filed off with a point file (fine emery paper will also do), but it is usually wise to replace the breaker point set, unless you have access to a condenser tester.

To replace the breaker points:

1. Remove the rotor.
2. Unsnap the point connector from the terminal at the side of the distributor.

Remove the retaining screw and lift out the point set.

3. Install the new point set, making sure that the pin of the bottom engages the hole in the breaker plate.

4. Install wire connector and the retaining screw (hand-tight).

5. Turn the fan belt or crankshaft pulley until the breaker arm rubbing block is on the high point of one of the cam lobes. This may seem at first a bit confusing, but it really isn't. The rotor rides on the distributor cam, down at the base of the cam by the breaker points. You will notice that the cam has high and low points. When the point rubbing block is on a high point of the distributor cam, the points open and fire. In order to check the gap, the points have to be open, so all your doing is turning the engine until one of the high points on the distributor cam opens the breaker points.

6. When they're open, slip a 0.016 (0.40 mm) in. feeler gauge between them. It should just slide through; if you're unsure about the opening size, try slipping a larger size in there, it shouldn't fit, and a smaller size should slide through very easily. If the gap is incorrect, insert a screwdriver into the point set notch and the two projections (knobs) on the breaker plate and twist the screwdriver into the point plate and twist the screwdriver to bring the gap to within the specifications (see the illustration).

7. When the gap is correct, tighten the retaining screw. After tightening the retaining screw, recheck the gap because sometimes it may slip out of adjustment when tightening the retaining screw.

8. Lubricate the distributor cam with a silicone grease. This is sometimes supplied with the new points sets; if not it can be purchased at any auto supply store.

9. The condenser is mounted on the outside of the distributor. Remove the mounting screw and the terminal block to replace the condenser.

10. Install the dust cover, rotor and distributor cap.

11. Check the dwell angle and ignition timing as outlined in the following sections.

IGNITION TIMING

CAUTION: *When performing this or any other operation with the engine running, be very careful of the alternator belt and pulleys. Make sure that your timing light wires don't interfere with the belt.*

Ignition timing is an important part of the tune-up. It is always adjusted after the points are gapped (dwell angle changed), since altering the dwell affects the timing. Three basic types of timing lights are available, the neon, the DC, and the AC powered. Of the three, the DC light is the most frequently used. The bright flash put out by the DC light makes the timing marks stand out on even the brightest of days. Another advantage of the DC light is that you don't need to be near an electrical outlet. Neon lights are available for a few dollars, but their weak flash makes it necessary to use them in a fairly dark work area. One neon light lead is attached to the spark plug and the other to the plug wire. The DC light attaches to the spark plug and the wire with an adapter and two clips and two clips attach to the battery posts for power. The AC unit is similar, except that the power cable is plugged into a house outlet.

1. Attach the timing light as outlined above or according to the manufacturer's instructions. Hook up a dwell/tachometer since you'll need an rpm indication for correct timing.

2. Locate the timing mark opening in the clutch or torque converter housing at the rear of the engine directly behind the distributor. The "OT" mark stands for TDC or 0° advance. The "3" mark designates 3° ATDC. Mark them with chalk so that they will be more visible. Don't disconnect the vacuum line.

Adjusting the point gap with a screwdriver

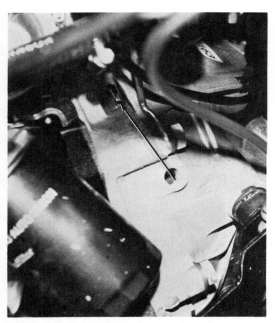

Timing mark opening and pointer (arrow)

3. Start the engine and allow it to reach the normal operating temperature. The engine should be running at normal idle speed.

4. The light should now be flashing when the 3° line (or 0/T if it's a '73), and the V-shaped pointer are aligned.

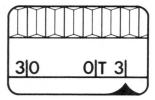

Timing marks must look like this when timing is correct for 1974–75 Foxes

Correct timing mark alignment for 1973 Foxes

5. If not, loosen the distributor hold-down bolt and rotate the distributor very slowly to align the marks.

6. Tighten the mounting nut when the ignition timing is correct.

7. Recheck the timing when the distributor is secured.

With the ignition timing correctly adjusted, the spark plugs will fire at the exact instant the piston is nearing the top of the compression stroke, thus providing maximum power and economy.

VALVE LASH

Because of the length of time between adjustments, and the complicated nature of the adjusting process, this is not considered a normal tune-up procedure. It is covered however, in Chapter 3, "Engine and Engine Rebuilding."

CARBURETOR

The carburetor used on 1973–74 Fox models is a Solex 32/35 DIDTA two-barrel unit with a vacuum-operated secondary barrel which opens only when accelerating. The results in good high rpm performance as well as smooth and economical low-speed operation. There are three adjusting screws on the carburetor, one of which, the screw on throttle linkage, is sealed at the factory and should not require further adjustment. The two screws which may be adjusted are the auxiliary mixture control idle speed; and the auxiliary fuel control screw which affects carbon monoxide content at idle.

Arrows showing the location of the auxiliary fuel control screw (top), and auxiliary mixture control screw (bottom)

Idle Speed Adjustment

1. Start the engine and run it until the normal operating temperature is reached.

2. Hook-up a tachometer to the engine and observe the idle speed.

3. If the idle speed differs from 925 rpm ±25 rpm, turn the auxiliary mixture control screw to correct it. Make sure that you are turning the correct screw as shown in the illustration. Do not mistake the auxiliary mixture control screw for the auxiliary fuel control.

Close up of the carburetor adjusting screws, the auxiliary mixture control screw (13), and the auxiliary fuel control screw (14)

Idle Mixture Adjustment

This adjustment should be performed if you have access to an accurate CO meter, otherwise leave it to your dealer or a service garage. Notice that the California auxiliary fuel control screw is in a different location.

ALL 1974 MODELS EXCEPT CALIFORNIA (WITHOUT AIR PUMP)

1. Run the engine until it reaches normal operating temperature.

2. Ignition timing should be correctly set at 3° ATDC.

3. Idle speed should be 925 ±25 rpm.

4. Adjust the CO level with the auxiliary fuel control screw to 1% ±0.6%.

Remove the air pump line at this point and plug it

1975 Fox CIS fuel injection unit

1974 CALIFORNIA MODELS
(WITH AIR PUMP)

1. Run the engine until it reaches normal operating temperature.

2. Disconnect the hose which connects the air injection pump and the air manifold at the pump and plug it.

3. Ignition timing should be adjusted to 3° ATDC and idle speed set at 925 rpm ±25 rpm.

4. Adjust the CO level with idle mixture screw to 1.5%.

5. Unplug and connect the air injection pump hose. The CO level should now fall below 1%.

NOTE: *Starting 1975, the Audi Fox is equipped with CIS (Continuous Injection System) fuel injection. The injector unit requires no adjustment as part of the normal tune-up. Any adjustment procedures will be found in the "Emission Control and Fuel System" chapter.*

Engine Tune-Up

Engine tune-up is a procedure performed to restore engine performance, deteriorated due to normal wear and loss of adjustment. The three major areas considered in a routine tune-up are compression, ignition, and carburetion, although valve adjustment may be included.

A tune-up is performed in three steps: *analysis*, in which it is determined whether normal wear is responsible for performance loss, and which parts require replacement or service; *parts replacement or service*; and *adjustment*, in which engine adjustments are returned to original specifications. Since the advent of emission control equipment, precision adjustment has become increasingly critical, in order to maintain pollutant emission levels.

Analysis

The procedures below are used to indicate where adjustments, parts service or replacement are necessary within the realm of a normal tune-up. If, following these tests, all systems appear to be functioning properly, proceed to the Troubleshooting Section for further diagnosis.

—Remove all spark plugs, noting the cylinder in which they were installed. Remove the air cleaner, and position the throttle and choke in the full open position. Disconnect the coil high tension lead from the coil and the distributor cap. Insert a compression gauge into the spark plug port of each cylinder, in succession, and crank the engine with

Maxi. Press. Lbs. Sq. In.	Min. Press. Lbs. Sq. In.	Max. Press. Lbs. Sq. In.	Min. Press. Lbs. Sq. In.
134	101	188	141
136	102	190	142
138	104	192	144
140	105	194	145
142	107	196	147
146	110	198	148
148	111	200	150
150	113	202	151
152	114	204	153
154	115	206	154
156	117	208	156
158	118	210	157
160	120	212	158
162	121	214	160
164	123	216	162
166	124	218	163
168	126	220	165
170	127	222	166
172	129	224	168
174	131	226	169
176	132	228	171
178	133	230	172
180	135	232	174
182	136	234	175
184	138	236	177
186	140	238	178

Compression pressure limits
© Buick Div. G.M. Corp.)

the starter to obtain the highest possible reading. Record the readings, and compare the highest to the lowest on the compression pressure limit chart. If the difference exceeds the limits on the chart, or if all readings are excessively low, proceed to a wet compression check (see Troubleshooting Section).

—Evaluate the spark plugs according to the spark plug chart in the Troubleshooting Section, and proceed as indicated in the chart.

—Remove the distributor cap, and inspect it inside and out for cracks and/or carbon tracks, and inside for excessive wear or burning of the rotor contacts. If any of these faults are evident, the cap must be replaced.

—Check the breaker points for burning, pitting or wear, and the contact heel resting on the distributor cam for excessive wear. If defects are noted, replace the entire breaker point set.

—Remove and inspect the rotor. If the contacts are burned or worn, or if the rotor is excessively loose on the distributor shaft (where applicable), the rotor must be replaced.

—Inspect the spark plug leads and the coil high tension lead for cracks or brittleness. If any of the wires appear defective, the entire set should be replaced.

—Check the air filter to ensure that it is functioning properly.

Parts Replacement and Service

The determination of whether to replace or service parts is at the mechanic's discretion; however, it is suggested that any parts in questionable condition be replaced rather than reused.

—Clean and regap, or replace, the spark plugs as needed. Lightly coat the threads with engine oil and install the plugs. CAUTION: *Do not over-torque taper-seat spark plugs, or plugs being installed in aluminum cylinder heads.*

SPARK PLUG TORQUE

Thread size	Cast-Iron Heads	Aluminum Heads
10 mm.	14	11
14 mm.	30	27
18 mm.	34*	32
7/8 in.—18	37	35

* 17 ft. lbs. for tapered plugs using no gaskets.

—If the distributor cap is to be reused, clean the inside with a dry rag, and remove corrosion from the rotor contact points with fine emery cloth. Remove the spark plug wires one by one, and clean the wire ends and the inside of the towers. If the boots are loose, they should be replaced.

If the cap is to be replaced, transfer the wires one by one, cleaning the wire ends and replacing the boots if necessary.

—If the original points are to remain in service, clean them lightly with emery cloth, lubricate the contact heel with grease specifically designed for this purpose. Rotate the crankshaft until the heel rests on a high point of the distributor cam, and adjust the point gap to specifications.

When replacing the points, remove the original points and condenser, and wipe out the inside of the distributor housing with a clean, dry rag. Lightly lubricate the contact heel and pivot point, and install the points and condenser. Rotate the crankshaft until the heel rests on a high point of the distributor cam, and adjust the point gap to specifications. NOTE: *Always replace the condenser when changing the points.*

—If the rotor is to be reused, clean the contacts with solvent. Do not alter the spring tension of the rotor center contact. Install the rotor and the distributor cap.

—Replace the coil high tension lead and/or the spark plug leads as necessary.

—Clean the carburetor using a spray solvent (e.g., Gumout Spray). Remove the varnish from the throttle bores, and clean the linkage. Disconnect and plug the fuel line, and run the engine until it runs out of fuel. Partially fill the float chamber with solvent, and reconnect the fuel line. In extreme cases, the jets can be pressure flushed by inserting a rubber plug into the float vent, running the spray nozzle through it, and spraying the solvent until it squirts out of the venturi fuel dump.

—Clean and tighten all wiring connections in the primary electrical circuit.

Additional Services

The following services *should* be performed in conjunction with a routine tune-up to ensure efficient performance.

—Inspect the battery and fill to the proper level with distilled water. Remove the cable clamps, clean clamps and posts thoroughly, coat the posts lightly with petroleum jelly, reinstall and tighten.

—Inspect all belts, replace and/or adjust as necessary.

—Test the PCV valve (if so equipped), and clean or replace as indicated. Clean all crankcase ventilation hoses, or replace if cracked or hardened.

—Adjust the valves (if necessary) to manufacturer's specifications.

Adjustments

—Connect a dwell-tachometer between the distributor primary lead and ground. Remove the distributor cap and rotor (unless equipped with Delco externally adjustable distributor). With the ignition off, crank the engine with a remote starter switch and measure the point dwell angle. Adjust the dwell angle to specifications. NOTE: *Increasing the gap decreases the dwell angle and vice-versa.* Install the rotor and distributor cap.

—Connect a timing light according to the manufacturer's specifications. Identify the proper timing marks with chalk or paint. NOTE: *Luminescent (day-glo) paint is excellent for this purpose.* Start the engine, and run it until it reaches operating temperature. Disconnect and plug any distributor vacuum lines, and adjust idle to the speed required to adjust timing, according to specifications. Loosen the distributor clamp and adjust timing to specifications by rotating the distributor in the engine. NOTE: *To advance timing, rotate distributor opposite normal direction of rotor rotation, and vice-versa.*

—Synchronize the throttles and mixture of multiple carburetors (if so equipped) according to procedures given in the individual car sections.

—Adjust the idle speed, mixture, and idle quality, as specified in the car sections. Final idle adjustments should be made with the air cleaner installed. CAUTION: *Due to strict emission control requirements on 1969 and later models, special test equipment (CO meter, SUN Tester) may be necessary to properly adjust idle mixture to specifications.*

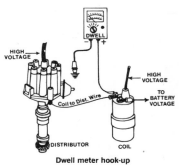

Dwell meter hook-up

Trouble-shooting

The following section is designed to aid in the rapid diagnosis of engine problems. The systematic format is used to diagnose problems ranging from engine starting difficulties to the need for engine overhaul. It is assumed that the user is equipped with basic hand tools and test equipment (tach-dwell meter, timing light, voltmeter, and ohmmeter).

Troubleshooting is divided into two sections. The first, *General Diagnosis*, is used to locate the problem area. In the second, *Specific Diagnosis*, the problem is systematically evaluated.

General Diagnosis

PROBLEM : Symptom	Begin diagnosis at Section Two, Number ———
Engine won't start :	
Starter doesn't turn	1.1, 2.1
Starter turns, engine doesn't	2.1
Starter turns engine very slowly	1.1, 2.4
Starter turns engine normally	3.1, 4.1
Starter turns engine very quickly	6.1
Engine fires intermittently	4.1
Engine fires consistently	5.1, 6.1
Engine runs poorly :	
Hard starting	3.1, 4.1, 5.1, 8.1
Rough idle	4.1, 5.1, 8.1
Stalling	3.1, 4.1, 5.1, 8.1
Engine dies at high speeds	4.1, 5.1
Hesitation (on acceleration from standing stop)	5.1, 8.1
Poor pickup	4.1, 5.1, 8.1
Lack of power	3.1, 4.1, 5.1, 8.1
Backfire through the carburetor	4.1, 8.1, 9.1
Backfire through the exhaust	4.1, 8.1, 9.1
Blue exhaust gases	6.1, 7.1
Black exhaust gases	5.1
Running on (after the ignition is shut off)	3.1, 8.1
Susceptible to moisture	4.1
Engine misfires under load	4.1, 7.1, 8.4, 9.1
Engine misfires at speed	4.1, 8.4
Engine misfires at idle	3.1, 4.1, 5.1, 7.1, 8.4

PROBLEM : Symptom	Probable Cause
Engine noises : ①	
Metallic grind while starting	Starter drive not engaging completely
Constant grind or rumble	*Starter drive not releasing, worn main bearings
Constant knock	Worn connecting rod bearings
Knock under load	Fuel octane too low, worn connecting rod bearings
Double knock	Loose piston pin
Metallic tap	*Collapsed or sticky valve lifter, excessive valve clearance, excessive end play in a rotating shaft
Scrape	*Fan belt contacting a stationary surface
Tick while starting	S.U. electric fuel pump (normal), starter brushes
Constant tick	*Generator brushes, shreaded fan belt
Squeal	*Improperly tensioned fan belt
Hiss or roar	*Steam escaping through a leak in the cooling system or the radiator overflow vent
Whistle	*Vacuum leak
Wheeze	Loose or cracked spark plug

①—It is extremely difficult to evaluate vehicle noises. While the above are general definitions of engine noises, those starred (*) should be considered as possibly originating elsewhere in the car. To aid diagnosis, the following list considers other potential sources of these sounds.

Metallic grind:
Throwout bearing; transmission gears, bearings, or synchronizers; differential bearings, gears; something metallic in contact with brake drum or disc.

Metallic tap:
U-joints; fan-to-radiator (or shroud) contact.

Scrape:
Brake shoe or pad dragging; tire to body contact; suspension contacting undercarriage or exhaust; something non-metallic contacting brake shoe or drum.

Tick:
Transmission gears; differential gears; lack of radio suppression; resonant vibration of body panels; windshield wiper motor or transmission; heater motor and blower.

Squeal:
Brake shoe or pad not fully releasing; tires (excessive wear, uneven wear, improper inflation); front or rear wheel alignment (most commonly due to improper toe-in).

Hiss or whistle:
Wind leaks (body or window); heater motor and blower fan.

Roar:
Wheel bearings; wind leaks (body and window).

Specific Diagnosis

This section is arranged so that following each test, instructions are given to proceed to another, until a problem is diagnosed.

INDEX

Group		Topic
1	*	Battery
2	*	Cranking system
3	*	Primary electrical system
4	*	Secondary electrical system
5	*	Fuel system
6	*	Engine compression
7	**	Engine vacuum
8	**	Secondary electrical system
9	**	Valve train
10	**	Exhaust system
11	**	Cooling system
12	**	Engine lubrication

*—The engine need not be running.
**—The engine must be running.

SAMPLE SECTION

Test and Procedure	Results and Indications	Proceed to
4.1—Check for spark: Hold each spark plug wire approximately ¼″ from ground with gloves or a heavy, dry rag. Crank the engine and observe the spark.	→ If no spark is evident: ————————→	4.2
	→ If spark is good in some cases: ——————→	4.3
	→ If spark is good in all cases: ————————→	4.6

DIAGNOSIS

Test and Procedure	Results and Indications	Proceed to
1.1—Inspect the battery visually for case condition (corrosion, cracks) and water level.	If case is cracked, replace battery:	1.4
	If the case is intact, remove corrosion with a solution of baking soda and water (CAUTION: *do not get the solution into the battery*), and fill with water:	1.2
1.2—Check the battery cable connections: Insert a screwdriver between the battery post and the cable clamp. Turn the headlights on high beam, and observe them as the screwdriver is gently twisted to ensure good metal to metal contact. **Testing battery cable connections using a screwdriver**	If the lights brighten, remove and clean the clamp and post; coat the post with petroleum jelly, install and tighten the clamp:	1.4
	If no improvement is noted:	1.3

1.3—Test the state of charge of the battery using an individual cell tester or hydrometer.			If indicated, charge the battery. NOTE: *If no obvious reason exists for the low state of charge (i.e., battery age, prolonged storage), the charging system should be tested:*

Spec. Grav. Reading	Charged Condition
1.260–1.280	Fully Charged
1.230–1.250	Three Quarter Charged
1.200–1.220	One Half Charged
1.170–1.190	One Quarter Charged
1.140–1.160	Just About Flat
1.110–1.130	All The Way Down

State of battery charge

Electrolyte temperature (° F)	Specific gravity correction	
+ 120	+.016	
	+.012	ADD to reading
+ 100	+.008	
	+.004	
+ 80	no correction	
	—.004	
+ 60	—.008	
	—.012	
+ 40	—.016	
	—.020	
+ 20	—.024	SUBTRACT from reading
	—.028	
0	—.032	
	—.036	
— 20	—.040	

The effect of temperature on the specific gravity of battery electrolyte

1.4

Test and Procedure	*Results and Indications*	*Proceed to*
1.4—Visually inspect battery cables for cracking, bad connection to ground, or bad connection to starter.	If necessary, tighten connections or replace the cables:	2.1

Tests in Group 2 are performed with coil high tension lead disconnected to prevent accidental starting.

Test and Procedure	*Results and Indications*	*Proceed to*
2.1—Test the starter motor and solenoid: Connect a jumper from the battery post of the solenoid (or relay) to the starter post of the solenoid (or relay).	If starter turns the engine normally:	2.2
	If the starter buzzes, or turns the engine very slowly:	2.4
	If no response, replace the solenoid (or relay).	3.1
	If the starter turns, but the engine doesn't, ensure that the flywheel ring gear is intact. If the gear is undamaged, replace the starter drive.	3.1
2.2—Determine whether ignition override switches are functioning properly (clutch start switch, neutral safety switch), by connecting a jumper across the switch(es), and turning the ignition switch to "start".	If starter operates, adjust or replace switch:	3.1
	If the starter doesn't operate:	2.3
2.3—Check the ignition switch "start" position: Connect a 12V test lamp between the starter post of the solenoid (or relay) and ground. Turn the ignition switch to the "start" position, and jiggle the key.	If the lamp doesn't light when the switch is turned, check the ignition switch for loose connections, cracked insulation, or broken wires. Repair or replace as necessary:	3.1
	If the lamp flickers when the key is jiggled, replace the ignition switch.	3.3

Checking the ignition switch "start" position

Test and Procedure	*Results and Indications*	*Proceed to*
2.4—Remove and bench test the starter, according to specifications in the car section.	If the starter does not meet specifications, repair or replace as needed:	3.1
	If the starter is operating properly:	2.5
2.5—Determine whether the engine can turn freely: Remove the spark plugs, and check for water in the cylinders. Check for water on the dipstick, or oil in the radiator. Attempt to turn the engine using an 18" flex drive and socket on the crankshaft pulley nut or bolt.	If the engine will turn freely only with the spark plugs out, and hydrostatic lock (water in the cylinders) is ruled out, check valve timing:	9.2
	If engine will not turn freely, and it is known that the clutch and transmission are free, the engine must be disassembled for further evaluation:	Next Chapter

Tests and Procedures	*Results and Indications*	*Proceed to*
3.1—Check the ignition switch "on" position: Connect a jumper wire between the distributor side of the coil and ground, and a 12V test lamp between the switch side of the coil and ground. Remove the high tension lead from the coil. Turn the ignition switch on and jiggle the key.	If the lamp lights:	3.2
	If the lamp flickers when the key is jiggled, replace the ignition switch:	3.3
	If the lamp doesn't light, check for loose or open connections. If none are found, remove the ignition switch and check for continuity. If the switch is faulty, replace it:	3.3

Checking the ignition switch "on" position

Tests and Procedures	*Results and Indications*	*Proceed to*
3.2—Check the ballast resistor or resistance wire for an open circuit, using an ohmmeter.	Replace the resistor or the resistance wire if the resistance is zero.	3.3
3.3—Visually inspect the breaker points for burning, pitting, or excessive wear. Gray coloring of the point contact surfaces is normal. Rotate the crankshaft until the contact heel rests on a high point of the distributor cam, and adjust the point gap to specifications.	If the breaker points are intact, clean the contact surfaces with fine emery cloth, and adjust the point gap to specifications. If pitted or worn, replace the points and condenser, and adjust the gap to specifications: NOTE: *Always lubricate the distributor cam according to manufacturer's recommendations when servicing the breaker points.*	3.4
3.4—Connect a dwell meter between the distributor primary lead and ground. Crank the engine and observe the point dwell angle.	If necessary, adjust the point dwell angle: NOTE: *Increasing the point gap decreases the dwell angle, and vice-versa.*	3.6
	If dwell meter shows little or no reading:	3.5

Dwell meter hook-up

Dwell angle

Tests and Procedures	*Results and Indications*	*Proceed to*
3.5—Check the condenser for short: Connect an ohmmeter across the condenser body and the pigtail lead.	If any reading other than infinite resistance is noted, replace the condenser:	3.6

Checking the condenser for short

Test and Procedure	Results and Indications	Proceed to
3.6—Test the coil primary resistance: Connect an ohmmeter across the coil primary terminals, and read the resistance on the low scale. Note whether an external ballast resistor or resistance wire is utilized.	Coils utilizing ballast resistors or resistance wires should have approximately 1.0Ω resistance; coils with internal resistors should have approximately 4.0Ω resistance. If values far from the above are noted, replace the coil:	4.1

Testing the coil primary resistance

Test and Procedure	Results and Indications	Proceed to
4.1—Check for spark: Hold each spark plug wire approximately $\frac{1}{4}$″ from ground with gloves or a heavy, dry rag. Crank the engine, and observe the spark.	If no spark is evident:	4.2
	If spark is good in some cylinders:	4.3
	If spark is good in all cylinders:	4.6
4.2—Check for spark at the coil high tension lead: Remove the coil high tension lead from the distributor and position it approximately $\frac{1}{4}$″ from ground. Crank the engine and observe spark. CAUTION: *This test should not be performed on cars equipped with transistorized ignition.*	If the spark is good and consistent:	4.3
	If the spark is good but intermittent, test the primary electrical system starting at 3.3:	3.3
	If the spark is weak or non-existent, replace the coil high tension lead, clean and tighten all connections and retest. If no improvement is noted:	4.4
4.3—Visually inspect the distributor cap and rotor for burned or corroded contacts, cracks, carbon tracks, or moisture. Also check the fit of the rotor on the distributor shaft (where applicable).	If moisture is present, dry thoroughly, and retest per 4.1:	4.1
	If burned or excessively corroded contacts, cracks, or carbon tracks are noted, replace the defective part(s) and retest per 4.1:	4.1
	If the rotor and cap appear intact, or are only slightly corroded, clean the contacts thoroughly (including the cap towers and spark plug wire ends) and retest per 4.1:	
	If the spark is good in all cases:	4.6
	If the spark is poor in all cases:	4.5
4.4—Check the coil secondary resistance: Connect an ohmmeter across the distributor side of the coil and the coil tower. Read the resistance on the high scale of the ohmmeter.	The resistance of a satisfactory coil should be between $4K\Omega$ and $10K\Omega$. If the resistance is considerably higher (i.e., $40K\Omega$) replace the coil, and retest per 4.1: NOTE: *This does not apply to high performance coils.*	4.1

Testing the coil secondary resistance

Test and Procedure	Results and Indications	Proceed to
4.5—Visually inspect the spark plug wires for cracking or brittleness. Ensure that no two wires are positioned so as to cause induction firing (adjacent and parallel). Remove each wire, one by one, and check resistance with an ohmmeter.	Replace any cracked or brittle wires. If any of the wires are defective, replace the entire set. Replace any wires with excessive resistance (over 8000Ω per foot for suppression wire), and separate any wires that might cause induction firing.	4.6
4.6—Remove the spark plugs, noting the cylinders from which they were removed, and evaluate according to the chart below.	See below.	See below.

	Condition	Cause	Remedy	Proceed to
	Electrodes eroded, light brown deposits.	Normal wear. Normal wear is indicated by approximately .001″ wear per 1000 miles.	Clean and regap the spark plug if wear is not excessive: Replace the spark plug if excessively worn:	4.7
	Carbon fouling (black, dry, fluffy deposits).	If present on one or two plugs:		
		Faulty high tension lead(s).	Test the high tension leads:	4.5
		Burnt or sticking valve(s).	Check the valve train: (Clean and regap the plugs in either case.)	9.1
		If present on most or all plugs: Overly rich fuel mixture, due to restricted air filter, improper carburetor adjustment, improper choke or heat riser adjustment or operation.	Check the fuel system:	5.1
	Oil fouling (wet black deposits)	Worn engine components. NOTE: *Oil fouling may occur in new or recently rebuilt engines until broken in.*	Check engine vacuum and compression: Replace with new spark plug	6.1
	Lead fouling (gray, black, tan, or yellow deposits, which appear glazed or cinderlike).	Combustion by-products.	Clean and regap the plugs: (Use plugs of a different heat range if the problem recurs.)	4.7

Condition	Cause	Remedy	Proceed to
Gap bridging (deposits lodged between the electrodes).	Incomplete combustion, or transfer of deposits from the combustion chamber.	Replace the spark plugs:	4.7
Overheating (burnt electrodes, and extremely white insulator with small black spots).	Ignition timing advanced too far.	Adjust timing to specifications:	8.2
	Overly lean fuel mixture.	Check the fuel system:	5.1
	Spark plugs not seated properly.	Clean spark plug seat and install a new gasket washer: (Replace the spark plugs in all cases.)	4.7
Fused spot deposits on the insulator.	Combustion chamber blow-by.	Clean and regap the spark plugs:	4.7
Pre-ignition (melted or severely burned electrodes, blistered or cracked insulators, or metallic deposits on the insulator).	Incorrect spark plug heat range.	Replace with plugs of the proper heat range:	4.7
	Ignition timing advanced too far.	Adjust timing to specifications:	8.2
	Spark plugs not being cooled efficiently.	Clean the spark plug seat, and check the cooling system:	11.1
	Fuel mixture too lean.	Check the fuel system:	5.1
	Poor compression.	Check compression:	6.1
	Fuel grade too low.	Use higher octane fuel:	4.7

Test and Procedure	Results and Indications	Proceed to
4.7—Determine the static ignition timing: Using the flywheel or crankshaft pulley timing marks as a guide, locate top dead center on the *compression* stroke of the No. 1 cylinder. Remove the distributor cap.	Adjust the distributor so that the rotor points toward the No. 1 tower in the distributor cap, and the points are just opening:	4.8
4.8—Check coil polarity: Connect a voltmeter negative lead to the coil high tension lead, and the positive lead to ground (NOTE: *reverse the hook-up for positive ground cars*). Crank the engine momentarily. **Checking coil polarity**	If the voltmeter reads up-scale, the polarity is correct:	5.1
	If the voltmeter reads down-scale, reverse the coil polarity (switch the primary leads):	5.1

Test and Procedure	Results and Indications	Proceed to
5.1—Determine that the air filter is functioning efficiently: Hold paper elements up to a strong light, and attempt to see light through the filter.	Clean permanent air filters in gasoline (or manufacturer's recommendation), and allow to dry. Replace paper elements through which light cannot be seen:	5.2
5.2—Determine whether a flooding condition exists: Flooding is identified by a strong gasoline odor, and excessive gasoline present in the throttle bore(s) of the carburetor.	If flooding is not evident:	5.3
	If flooding is evident, permit the gasoline to dry for a few moments and restart.	
	If flooding doesn't recur:	5.6
	If flooding is persistant:	5.5
5.3—Check that fuel is reaching the carburetor: Detach the fuel line at the carburetor inlet. Hold the end of the line in a cup (not styrofoam), and crank the engine.	If fuel flows smoothly:	5.6
	If fuel doesn't flow (NOTE: *Make sure that there is fuel in the tank*), or flows erratically:	5.4
5.4—Test the fuel pump: Disconnect all fuel lines from the fuel pump. Hold a finger over the input fitting, crank the engine (with electric pump, turn the ignition or pump on); and feel for suction.	If suction is evident, blow out the fuel line to the tank with low pressure compressed air until bubbling is heard from the fuel filler neck. Also blow out the carburetor fuel line (both ends disconnected):	5.6
	If no suction is evident, replace or repair the fuel pump:	5.6
	NOTE: *Repeated oil fouling of the spark plugs, or a no-start condition, could be the result of a ruptured vacuum booster pump diaphragm, through which oil or gasoline is being drawn into the intake manifold (where applicable).*	
5.5—Check the needle and seat: Tap the carburetor in the area of the needle and seat.	If flooding stops, a gasoline additive (e.g., Gumout) will often cure the problem:	5.6
	If flooding continues, check the fuel pump for excessive pressure at the carburetor (according to specifications). If the pressure is normal, the needle and seat must be removed and checked, and/or the float level adjusted:	5.6
5.6—Test the accelerator pump by looking into the throttle bores while operating the throttle.	If the accelerator pump appears to be operating normally:	5.7
	If the accelerator pump is not operating, the pump must be reconditioned. Where possible, service the pump with the carburetor(s) installed on the engine. If necessary, remove the carburetor. Prior to removal:	5.7
5.7—Determine whether the carburetor main fuel system is functioning: Spray a commercial starting fluid into the carburetor while attempting to start the engine.	If the engine starts, runs for a few seconds, and dies:	5.8
	If the engine doesn't start:	6.1

Test and Procedures	Results and Indications	Proceed to
5.8—Uncommon fuel system malfunctions: See below:	If the problem is solved: If the problem remains, remove and recondition the carburetor.	6.1

Condition	Indication	Test	Usual Weather Conditions	Remedy
Vapor lock	Car will not restart shortly after running.	Cool the components of the fuel system until the engine starts.	Hot to very hot	Ensure that the exhaust manifold heat control valve is operating. Check with the vehicle manufacturer for the recommended solution to vapor lock on the model in question.
Carburetor icing	Car will not idle, stalls at low speeds.	Visually inspect the throttle plate area of the throttle bores for frost.	High humidity, 32-40° F.	Ensure that the exhaust manifold heat control valve is operating, and that the intake manifold heat riser is not blocked.
Water in the fuel	Engine sputters and stalls; may not start.	Pump a small amount of fuel into a glass jar. Allow to stand, and inspect for droplets or a layer of water.	High humidity, extreme temperature changes.	For droplets, use one or two cans of commercial gas dryer (Dry Gas) For a layer of water, the tank must be drained, and the fuel lines blown out with compressed air.

Test and Procedure	Results and Indications	Proceed to
6.1—Test engine compression: Remove all spark plugs. Insert a compression gauge into a spark plug port, crank the engine to obtain the maximum reading, and record.	If compression is within limits on all cylinders:	7.1
	If gauge reading is extremely low on all cylinders:	6.2
	If gauge reading is low on one or two cylinders: (If gauge readings are identical and low on two or more adjacent cylinders, the head gasket must be replaced.)	6.2

Testing compression
(© Chevrolet Div. G.M. Corp.)

Compression pressure limits
(© Buick Div. G.M. Corp.)

Maxi. Press. Lbs. Sq. In.	Min. Press. Lbs. Sq. In.	Maxi. Press. Lbs. Sq. In.	Min. Press. Lbs. Sq. In.	Max. Press. Lbs. Sq. In.	Min. Press. Lbs. Sq. In.	Max. Press. Lbs. Sq. In.	Min. Press. Lbs. Sq. In.
134	101	162	121	188	141	214	160
136	102	164	123	190	142	216	162
138	104	166	124	192	144	218	163
140	105	168	126	194	145	220	165
142	107	170	127	196	147	222	166
146	110	172	129	198	148	224	168
148	111	174	131	200	150	226	169
150	113	176	132	202	151	228	171
152	114	178	133	204	153	230	172
154	115	180	135	206	154	232	174
156	117	182	136	208	156	234	175
158	118	184	138	210	157	236	177
160	120	186	140	212	158	238	178

Test and Procedure	*Results and Indications*	*Proceed to*
6.2—Test engine compression (wet): Squirt approximately 30 cc. of engine oil into each cylinder, and retest per 6.1.	If the readings improve, worn or cracked rings or broken pistons are indicated:	Next Chapter
	If the readings do not improve, burned or excessively carboned valves or a jumped timing chain are indicated:	7.1
	NOTE: *A jumped timing chain is often indicated by difficult cranking.*	
7.1—Perform a vacuum check of the engine: Attach a vacuum gauge to the intake manifold beyond the throttle plate. Start the engine, and observe the action of the needle over the range of engine speeds.	See below.	See below

	Reading	*Indications*	*Proceed to*
	Steady, from 17-22 in. Hg.	Normal.	8.1
	Low and steady.	Late ignition or valve timing, or low compression:	6.1
	Very low	Vacuum leak:	7.2
	Needle fluctuates as engine speed increases.	Ignition miss, blown cylinder head gasket, leaking valve or weak valve spring:	6.1, 8.3
	Gradual drop in reading at idle.	Excessive back pressure in the exhaust system:	10.1
	Intermittent fluctuation at idle.	Ignition miss, sticking valve:	8.3, 9.1
	Drifting needle.	Improper idle mixture adjustment, carburetors not synchronized (where applicable), or minor intake leak. Synchronize the carburetors, adjust the idle, and retest. If the condition persists:	7.2
	High and steady.	Early ignition timing:	8.2

Test and Procedure	Results and Indications	Proceed to
7.2—Attach a vacuum gauge per 7.1, and test for an intake manifold leak. Squirt a small amount of oil around the intake manifold gaskets, carburetor gaskets, plugs and fittings. Observe the action of the vacuum gauge.	If the reading improves, replace the indicated gasket, or seal the indicated fitting or plug: If the reading remains low:	8.1 7.3
7.3—Test all vacuum hoses and accessories for leaks as described in 7.2. Also check the carburetor body (dashpots, automatic choke mechanism, throttle shafts) for leaks in the same manner.	If the reading improves, service or replace the offending part(s): If the reading remains low:	8.1 6.1
8.1—Check the point dwell angle: Connect a dwell meter between the distributor primary wire and ground. Start the engine, and observe the dwell angle from idle to 3000 rpm.	If necessary, adjust the dwell angle. NOTE: *Increasing the point gap reduces the dwell angle and vice-versa.* If the dwell angle moves outside specifications as engine speed increases, the distributor should be removed and checked for cam accuracy, shaft end-play and concentricity, bushing wear, and adequate point arm tension (NOTE: *Most of these items may be checked with the distributor installed in the engine, using an oscilloscope*):	8.2
8.2—Connect a timing light (per manufacturer's recommendation) and check the dynamic ignition timing. Disconnect and plug the vacuum hose(s) to the distributor if specified, start the engine, and observe the timing marks at the specified engine speed.	If the timing is not correct, adjust to specifications by rotating the distributor in the engine: (Advance timing by rotating distributor opposite normal direction of rotor rotation, retard timing by rotating distributor in same direction as rotor rotation.)	8.3
8.3—Check the operation of the distributor advance mechanism(s): To test the mechanical advance, disconnect all but the mechanical advance, and observe the timing marks with a timing light as the engine speed is increased from idle. If the mark moves smoothly, without hesitation, it may be assumed that the mechanical advance is functioning properly. To test vacuum advance and/or retard systems, alternately crimp and release the vacuum line, and observe the timing mark for movement. If movement is noted, the system is operating.	If the systems are functioning: If the systems are not functioning, remove the distributor, and test on a distributor tester:	8.4 8.4
8.4—Locate an ignition miss: With the engine running, remove each spark plug wire, one by one, until one is found that doesn't cause the engine to roughen and slow down.	When the missing cylinder is identified:	4.1

Test and Procedure	*Results and Indications*	*Proceed to*
9.1—Evaluate the valve train: Remove the valve cover, and ensure that the valves are adjusted to specifications. A mechanic's stethoscope may be used to aid in the diagnosis of the valve train. By pushing the probe on or near push rods or rockers, valve noise often can be isolated. A timing light also may be used to diagnose valve problems. Connect the light according to manufacturer's recommendations, and start the engine. Vary the firing moment of the light by increasing the engine speed (and therefore the ignition advance), and moving the trigger from cylinder to cylinder. Observe the movement of each valve.	See below	See below

Observation	*Probable Cause*	*Remedy*	*Proceed to*
Metallic tap heard through the stethoscope.	Sticking hydraulic lifter or excessive valve clearance.	Adjust valve. If tap persists, remove and replace the lifter:	10.1
Metallic tap through the stethoscope, able to push the rocker arm (lifter side) down by hand.	Collapsed valve lifter.	Remove and replace the lifter:	10.1
Erratic, irregular motion of the valve stem.*	Sticking valve, burned valve.	Recondition the valve and/or valve guide:	Next Chapter
Eccentric motion of the pushrod at the rocker arm.*	Bent pushrod.	Replace the pushrod:	10.1
Valve retainer bounces as the valve closes.*	Weak valve spring or damper.	Remove and test the spring and damper. Replace if necessary:	10.1

*—When observed with a timing light.

Test and Procedure	*Results and Indications*	*Proceed to*
9.2—Check the valve timing: Locate top dead center of the No. 1 piston, and install a degree wheel or tape on the crankshaft pulley or damper with zero corresponding to an index mark on the engine. Rotate the crankshaft in its direction of rotation, and observe the opening of the No. 1 cylinder intake valve. The opening should correspond with the correct mark on the degree wheel according to specifications.	If the timing is not correct, the timing cover must be removed for further investigation:	

Test and Procedure	Results and Indications	Proceed to
10.1—Determine whether the exhaust manifold heat control valve is operating: Operate the valve by hand to determine whether it is free to move. If the valve is free, run the engine to operating temperature and observe the action of the valve, to ensure that it is opening.	If the valve sticks, spray it with a suitable solvent, open and close the valve to free it, and retest. If the valve functions properly: If the valve does not free, or does not operate, replace the valve:	10.2 10.2
10.2—Ensure that there are no exhaust restrictions: Visually inspect the exhaust system for kinks, dents, or crushing. Also note that gasses are flowing freely from the tailpipe at all engine speeds, indicating no restriction in the muffler or resonator.	Replace any damaged portion of the system:	11.1
11.1—Visually inspect the fan belt for glazing, cracks, and fraying, and replace if necessary. Tighten the belt so that the longest span has approximately ½″ play at its midpoint under thumb pressure.	Replace or tighten the fan belt as necessary:	11.2

Checking the fan belt tension
(© Nissan Motor Co. Ltd.)

Test and Procedure	Results and Indications	Proceed to
11.2—Check the fluid level of the cooling system.	If full or slightly low, fill as necessary: If extremely low:	11.5 11.3
11.3—Visually inspect the external portions of the cooling system (radiator, radiator hoses, thermostat elbow, water pump seals, heater hoses, etc.) for leaks. If none are found, pressurize the cooling system to 14-15 psi.	If cooling system holds the pressure: If cooling system loses pressure rapidly, reinspect external parts of the system for leaks under pressure. If none are found, check dipstick for coolant in crankcase. If no coolant is present, but pressure loss continues: If coolant is evident in crankcase, remove cylinder head(s), and check gasket(s). If gaskets are intact, block and cylinder head(s) should be checked for cracks or holes. If the gasket(s) is blown, replace, and purge the crankcase of coolant: NOTE: *Occasionally, due to atmospheric and driving conditions, condensation of water can occur in the crankcase. This causes the oil to appear milky white. To remedy, run the engine until hot, and change the oil and oil filter.*	11.5 11.4 12.6

Test and Procedure	*Results and Indication*	*Proceed to*
11.4—Check for combustion leaks into the cooling system: Pressurize the cooling system as above. Start the engine, and observe the pressure gauge. If the needle fluctuates, remove each spark plug wire, one by one, noting which cylinder(s) reduce or eliminate the fluctuation. **Radiator pressure tester** (© American Motors Corp.)	Cylinders which reduce or eliminate the fluctuation, when the spark plug wire is removed, are leaking into the cooling system. Replace the head gasket on the affected cylinder bank(s).	
11.5—Check the radiator pressure cap: Attach a radiator pressure tester to the radiator cap (wet the seal prior to installation). Quickly pump up the pressure, noting the point at which the cap releases. **Testing the radiator pressure cap** (© American Motors Corp.)	If the cap releases within ± 1 psi of the specified rating, it is operating properly: If the cap releases at more than ± 1 psi of the specified rating, it should be replaced:	11.6 11.6
11.6—Test the thermostat: Start the engine cold, remove the radiator cap, and insert a thermometer into the radiator. Allow the engine to idle. After a short while, there will be a sudden, rapid increase in coolant temperature. The temperature at which this sharp rise stops is the thermostat opening temperature.	If the thermostat opens at or about the specified temperature: If the temperature doesn't increase: (If the temperature increases slowly and gradually, replace the thermostat.)	11.7 11.7
11.7—Check the water pump: Remove the thermostat elbow and the thermostat, disconnect the coil high tension lead (to prevent starting), and crank the engine momentarily.	If coolant flows, replace the thermostat and retest per 11.6: If coolant doesn't flow, reverse flush the cooling system to alleviate any blockage that might exist. If system is not blocked, and coolant will not flow, recondition the water pump.	11.6 —
12.1—Check the oil pressure gauge or warning light: If the gauge shows low pressure, or the light is on, for no obvious reason, remove the oil pressure sender. Install an accurate oil pressure gauge and run the engine momentarily.	If oil pressure builds normally, run engine for a few moments to determine that it is functioning normally, and replace the sender. If the pressure remains low: If the pressure surges: If the oil pressure is zero:	— 12.2 12.3 12.3

Test and Procedure	Results and Indications	Proceed to
12.2—Visually inspect the oil: If the oil is watery or very thin, milky, or foamy, replace the oil and oil filter.	If the oil is normal:	12.3
	If after replacing oil the pressure remains low:	12.3
	If after replacing oil the pressure becomes normal:	—
12.3—Inspect the oil pressure relief valve and spring, to ensure that it is not sticking or stuck. Remove and thoroughly clean the valve, spring, and the valve body.	If the oil pressure improves:	—
	If no improvement is noted:	12.4
12.4—Check to ensure that the oil pump is not cavitating (sucking air instead of oil): See that the crankcase is neither over nor underfull, and that the pickup in the sump is in the proper position and free from sludge.	Fill or drain the crankcase to the proper capacity, and clean the pickup screen in solvent if necessary. If no improvement is noted:	12.5
12.5—Inspect the oil pump drive and the oil pump:	If the pump drive or the oil pump appear to be defective, service as necessary and retest per 12.1:	12.1
	If the pump drive and pump appear to be operating normally, the engine should be disassembled to determine where blockage exists:	Next Chapter
12.6—Purge the engine of ethylene glycol coolant: Completely drain the crankcase and the oil filter. Obtain a commercial butyl cellosolve base solvent, designated for this purpose, and follow the instructions precisely. Following this, install a new oil filter and refill the crankcase with the proper weight oil. The next oil and filter change should follow shortly thereafter (1000 miles).		

Oil pressure relief valve
(© British Leyland Motors)

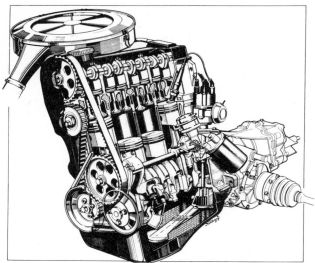

Chapter Three

Engine and Engine Rebuilding

Engine Electrical

DISTRIBUTOR

The Fox distributor is a conventional, single breaker point unit. It incorporates both centrifugal and vacuum ignition timing mechanisms. Centrifugal advance is controlled by two weights located beneath the breaker plate. As engine speed increases, centrifugal force moves the weights out from the distributor shaft and advances the ignition by changing the position of the cam in relation to the shaft. This advanced positioning of the cam will then open the breaker points sooner and ignite the air/fuel mixture quickly enough in relation to piston speed. Centrifugal advance is necessary because as engine speed increases, the time period available to ignite the mixture decreases. At idle speed, the Fox ignition setting is 3° ATDC. This is adequate for the spark plug to ignite the mixture at 925 rpm, but not at say, 2500 rpm. The weights, governed by springs, move out at a predetermined rate to advance the timing to match the engine speed.

Centrifugal advance is not completely sufficient to provide the proper advance under all conditions, and so we also have vacuum advance/retard. Under light load conditions, such as very gradual acceleration and low speed cruising, the throttle opening is not sufficient to draw enough air/fuel mixture into the cylinder. Vacuum advance is used to provide the extra spark advance needed to ignite the smaller mixture. The round can on the side of the distributor is the vacuum advance/retard unit. The rubber hose supplies vacuum from the intake manifold to draw on the diaphragm in the unit which is connected by a link to the breaker plate in the distributor. Under part-throttle operation, the vacuum advance moves the breaker plate as necessary to provide the correct advance for efficient operation. At idle, the vacuum retard unit retards the timing to reduce exhaust emission.

The distributor is gear driven by an intermediate shaft which also drives the fuel pump. The distributor shaft also turns the oil pump. The Fox distributor is located near the rear of the engine on the left-side and is easily accessible.

Removal and Installation

NOTE: *Aside from replacing the cap, rotor, breaker points, and the condenser, refer all distributor repair to a Audi dealer or ignition specialty shop. They are equipped with a distributor test machine which permits diagnosis of any problems.*

1. Disconnect the coil high-tension wire from the distributor. This is the wire which goes into the center of the cap.

2. Detach the smaller primary wire which also connects from the coil to the distributor.

3. Unsnap the clips and remove the distributor cap. Position it out of the way.

4. Using the fan belt or the crankshaft pulley nut, turn the engine until the rotor aligns with the index mark on the outer edge of the distributor. This is the No. 1 position. Scribe a mark on the bottom of the distributor housing and its mounting flange on the engine. This is extra insurance that we'll get the distributor back in correctly.

5. Loosen and remove the hex bolt and lift off the retaining flange. Lift the distributor straight out of the engine.

If the engine has not been disturbed while the distributor was out i.e., the crankshaft was not turned, then reinstall the distributor in the reverse order of removal. Carefully align the scribe marks.

If the engine has been rotated while the distributor was out, then proceed as follows:

1. Turn the crankshaft so that the No. 1 piston is on its compression stroke and the OT timing marks are aligned with the V-shaped pointer.

2. Turn the distributor so that the rotor points approximately 15° before the No. 1 cylinder position on the distributor.

Rotor aligned properly for replacement of the distributor when timing has been disturbed

3. Insert the distributor into the engine block. If the oil pump drive doesn't engage, remove the distributor and, using a long screwdriver, turn the pump shaft so that it is parallel to the centerline of the crankshaft.

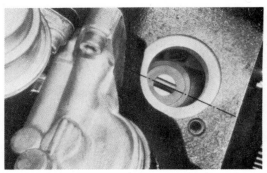

Oil pump shaft aligned parallel to the crankshaft for distributor installation

4. Install the distributor, aligning the matchmarks. Tighten the flange retaining nut.

5. Install the cap. Adjust the ignition timing as outlined in Chapter 2.

Firing Order

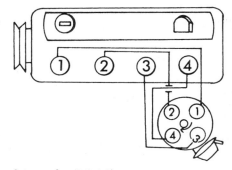

Fox firing order (1-3-4-2)

ALTERNATOR

The alternator, which is driven off the engine by a belt, supplies a steady current to the battery to enable it to provide power to the electrical systems of the car. To prevent the current to the battery from fluctuating with engine rpm, a voltage regulator is used which prevents power surges. Fuses are also used in the electrical system to prevent damage if there is an overload.

Alternator Precautions

The Fox is equipped with an alternating current (AC) generators (alternators). Unlike the direct current (DC) generators used in many older cars, there are several precautions which must be strictly observed in order to avoid damaging the unit. They are:

1. Reversing the battery connections will result in damage to the diodes.

2. Booster batteries should be connected from negative to negative, and positive to positive.

3. Never use a fast charger as a booster to start cars with AC circuits.

4. When servicing the battery with a fast charger, always disconnect the car battery cables.

5. Never attempt to polarize an AC generator.

6. Avoid long soldering times when replacing diodes or transistors. Prolonged heat is damaging to AC generators.

7. Do not use test lamps of more than 12 volts (V) for checking Diode continuity.

8. Do not short across or ground any of the terminals on the AC generator.

9. The polarity of the battery, generator, and regulator must be matched and considered before making any electrical connections within the system.

10. Never operate the AC generator on an open circuit. Make sure that all connections within the circuit are clean and tight.

11. Disconnect the battery terminals when performing any service on the electrical system. This will eliminate the possibility of accidental reversal of polarity.

12. Disconnect the battery ground cable if arc welding is to be done on any part of the car.

Removal and Installation

The Fox alternator and voltage regulator are combined in one housing. No voltage adjustment can be made with this unit. As with the distributor, repairs to the alternator should be made by an authorized dealer. The regulator can be replaced without removing the alternator, just unbolt it from the rear.

1. Disconnect the battery cables.

2. Remove the multiconnector retaining bracket and unplug the connector from the rear of the alternator.

3. Loosen and remove the top mounting nut and bolt.

4. Insert a long hex socket of the proper size through the timing belt cover. It is not necessary to remove the cover. Then loosen the lower mounting bolt.

5. Slide the alternator over and remove the alternator belt.

6. Remove the lower nut and belt. Don't lose the spacers or rubber isolators as they will be reused.

7. Remove the alternator.

NOTE: *Remember when installing the alternator that it is not necessary to polarize the AC generator system.*

8. Install the alternator with the lower bolt. Don't tighten it at this point.

9. Fit the alternator belt over the pulleys.

10. Loosely install the top mounting bolt and pivot the alternator over until the belt is correctly tensioned as explained in the next procedure.

11. Finally tighten the top and bottom bolts to 14 ft lbs.

12. Connect the alternator and battery wires.

Belt Replacement and Tensioning

1. Loosen the top alternator mounting bolt.

2. Using a hex socket inserted through the timing belt cover (it's not necessary to remove the cover), loosen the lower mounting bolt.

3. Using a pry bar, such as a large screwdriver or ratchet handle, slide the alternator over and remove the belt. Be careful not to damage the alternator with the prying device.

4. Slip the new belt over the pulleys.

5. Pry the alternator over until the belt deflection midway between the crankshaft pulley and the alternator pulley is $\frac{3}{8}$–$\frac{9}{16}$ in. (10–15 mm).

6. Securely tighten the mounting bolts.

NOTE: *The arrow on the alternator fan faces in the direction of rotation. Make sure that the arrow is facing in the proper direction before proceeding any farther.*

STARTER

The starter converts electrical energy from the battery into mechanical energy which then turns the engine over so that the plugs can ignite the air/fuel mixture in the cylinders and start the combustion process in the engine.

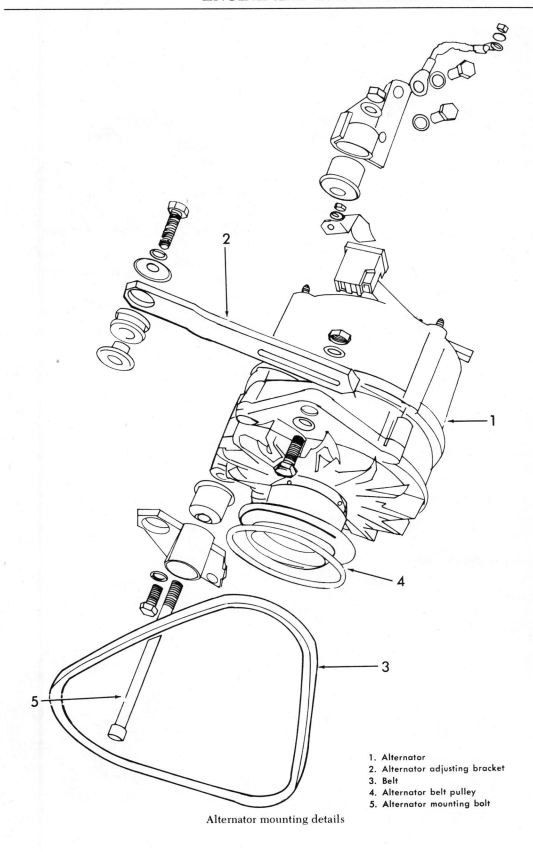

1. Alternator
2. Alternator adjusting bracket
3. Belt
4. Alternator belt pulley
5. Alternator mounting bolt

Alternator mounting details

Removal and Installation

1. Disconnect the battery ground cable.

2. Jack up the right front of the car and support with a sturdy jack stand.

3. Number and tag with tape and then disconnect the two small wires from the starter solenoid. One wire connects to the ignition coil and the second to the ignition switch through the wiring harness.

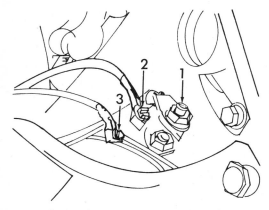

Starter electrical connections—(A) solenoid, (B) coil, (C) positive battery cable

1. **Battery cable**   2. **To ignition coil**   3. **To wiring harness**

4. Disconnect the large cable, which is the positive battery cable, from the solenoid.

5. Remove the three starter retaining nuts.

Starter retaining nuts (arrows)

6. Unscrew the socket head bolt. Pull the starter straight out and to the front.

7. Installation of the starter is carried out in reverse order of removal.

Overhaul

Use the following procedure to replace brushes or starter drive.

1. Remove the solenoid as outlined below.

2. Remove the end bearing cap.

3. Loosen both of the long housing screws.

Starter housing screws and lockwasher

4. Remove the lockwasher and space washers.

5. Remove the long housing screws and remove the end cover of the starter.

6. Pull the two field coil brushes out of the brush housing.

7. Remove the brush housing assembly.

8. Loosen the nut on the solenoid housing, remove the sealing disc, and remove the solenoid operating lever.

9. Loosen the large screws on the side of the starter body and remove the field coil along with the brushes.

NOTE: *If the brushes require replacement, the field coil and brushes and/or the brush housing and its brushes must be replaced as a unit. Have the*

Starter brush connected (arrow)

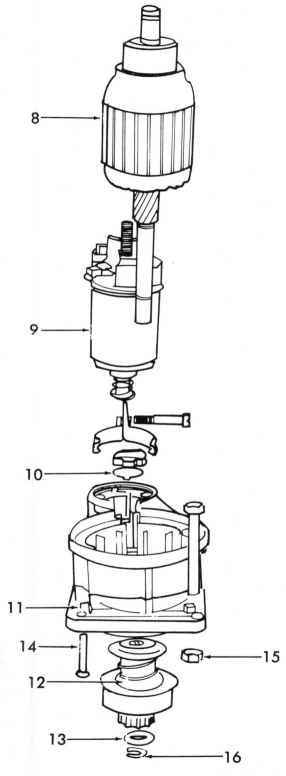
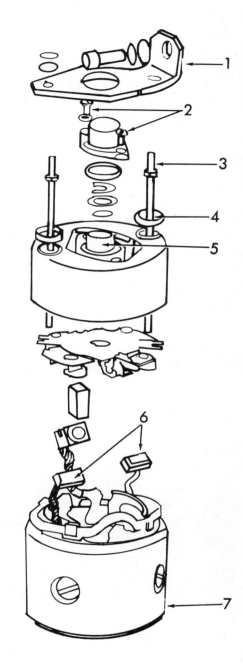

1. Mounting bracket
2. End cap screws
3. Housing screws
4. Cupped washer
5. End plate bushing
6. Brushes
7. Field coil housing
8. Armature
9. Solenoid
10. Disc
11. Mounting housing
12. Drive pinion
13. Stop ring
14. Solenoid bolt
15. Starter bolt and nut
16. Circlip

Exploded view of starter

armature commutator turned at a machine shop if it is out-of-round, scored, or grooved.

10. If the starter drive is being replaced, push the stop ring down and remove the circlip on the end of the shaft. Remove the stop ring and remove the drive.

11. Assembly of the starter is carried out in reverse order of disassembly. Use a gear puller to install the stop ring in its groove. Use a new circlip on the shaft.

Solenoid Replacement

The starter solenoid is a magnetic device which employs the small current supplied by the starting switch circuit of the ignition switch. This magnetic action moves a plunger which mechanically engages the starter and electrically closes a heavier switch which connects it to the battery. With the circuit complete, the starter engages.

1. Remove the starter.
2. Remove the nut which secures the connector strip on the end of the solenoid.
3. Take out the two retaining screws on the mounting bracket and withdraw the solenoid after it has been unhooked from the operating lever.

Removing the solenoid from the starter

4. Installation is the reverse of removal. In order to facilitate engagement of the lever, the pinion should be pulled out as far as possible when inserting the solenoid.

BATTERY

The battery on the 1973–74 Foxes is located in the engine compartment, on the right-side, near the firewall. On some early 1975 Fox sedans, the battery is lo-

cated in the trunk, on the left-side. Later '75s have the battery in back to the engine compartment.

This larger distance between the battery and the starter will drain the battery's power more quickly than if the battery was mounted in the engine compartment, so that it is especially important to periodically check on the battery condition as shown in Chapter 1, "General Information and Maintenance." Also on those models with the battery located in the trunk, be sure not to disturb the fuel pump ground wire which is connected directly to the battery. If the battery must be serviced for any reason, make sure that this wire is not disturbed.

Removal and Installation

CAUTION: *Battery electrolyte (acid) is highly corrosive and can damage both you and the paintwork. Be careful when lifting the battery in and out of the engine compartment.*

1. Disconnect the positive and negative battery cables.
2. Put on heavy work gloves.
3. Loosen the retaining clamp bolt and remove the clamp.
4. Disconnect the small electrical lead for the computor sensor.
5. Lift the battery carefully out of the tray.
6. Clean all corrosion deposits from the battery tray and the retaining plate. Spray them with rust preventative paint.
7. Install the battery in reverse order of removal. Polish the inside of the cables and give them a coat of petroleum jelly before installation.

Engine Mechanical

DESIGN

The Fox engine is an inline four-cylinder with single overhead camshaft. The engine is inclined 20° to the right. The center of gravity is in front of the axle, thereby providing lighter steering and better handling. The crankshaft runs in five bearings with thrust being taken on the center bearing. The cylinder block is cast iron. A steel reinforced belt drives the intermediate shaft and camshaft. The intermediate shaft drives the oil pump, distributor, and fuel pump.

The cylinder head is lightweight aluminum alloy. The intake and exhaust manifolds are mounted on the same side of the cylinder head. The valves are opened and closed by the camshaft lobes operating on cupped cam followers which fit over the valves and springs. This design results in lighter valve train weight and fewer moving parts. The Fox engine combines low maintenance and high power output along with low emissions and excellent fuel mileage.

General Engine Specifications

Year	Engine Displacement Cu in. (cc)	Carbu- retor Type	Horse- power @ rpm	Torque @ rpm (ft lbs)	Bore x Stroke (in.)	Compres- sion Ratio	Oil Pressure @ rpm (psi)
1973– 74	89.7 (1,471)	2 bbl Solex	75 @ 6000	82 @ 4000	3.01 x 3.15	8.2 : 1	7.1–21.3 @ idle
1975	97.0 (1,588)	CIS①	81 @ 5800 (79 in Calif.)	90.4 @ 3300	3.13 x 3.15	8.0 : 1	9–min 100–max

① CIS—Continuous Injection System (fuel injection)

Engine Codes

1973	1470 cc (89.7 cu in.)	ZD (manual trans)
		ZE (automatic trans)
1974	1490 cc (89.7 cu in.)	XW (manual trans)
		XV (automatic trans)
		XZ (manual trans, Calif.)
		XY (automatic trans, Calif.)
1975	1588 cc (96.8 cu in.)	YG (manual trans, all)
		YH (automatic trans, all)

Valve Specifications

Seat Angle (deg)	Spring Test Pressure (lbs @ in.)	Stem-to-Guide Clearance (in.)		Stem Diameter (in.)	
		Intake	Exhaust	Intake	Exhaust
45	96–106 @ 0.916①	0.001– 0.002	0.001– 0.002	0.314	0.313

① Outer spring; inner spring test pressure is 46–51 lbs @ 0.719 in.

NOTE: *Valve guides are removable.*

Crankshaft and Connecting Rod Specifications

All measurements are given in inches

Crankshaft				Connecting Rod		
Main Brg Journal Dia	Main Brg Oil Clearance	Shaft End-Play	Thrust on No.	Journal Diameter	Oil Clearance	Side Clearance
2.160	0.001–0.003	0.003–0.007	3	1.8110	0.0011–0.0034	0.010

Piston and Ring Specifications

All measurements are given in inches

	Ring Gap			Ring Side Clearance		
Piston Clearance	Top Compression	Bottom Compression	Oil Control	Top Compression	Bottom Compression	Oil Control
0.001	0.039	0.039	0.039	0.006	0.006	0.006

NOTE: *Three oversizes of pistons are available to accommodate overbores up to 0.040 in.*

Torque Specifications

(All readings in ft lbs)

Cylinder Head Bolts	Rod Bearing Bolts	Main Bearing Bolts	Crankshaft Pulley Bolt	Flywheel-To-Crankshaft Bolts	Manifold	
					In	Ex
54 cold 61 hot	25–33 ①	47	58	36	18	17

① Use new bolts

ENGINE REMOVAL AND INSTALLATION

1. Remove the air cleaner assembly together with the heated air intake unit and the crankcase vent hose.

2. Remove the retaining spring at the hook on the accelerator cable, then disconnect the cable from its support bracket.

3. Pull off the wire from the idle cut-off valve on the carburetor.

4. Disconnect the wires from the ignition coil (see the illustration) and from the oil pressure and temperature switch.

5. Loosen the clutch cable adjusting nuts and remove the cable.

6. Disconnect the outlet line at the fuel pump and plug the line to avoid spilling gas; remove the multipole connector plug at the back of the alternator, pull it out of the clip on the radiator shroud and move it out of the way.

Ignition coil (top), oil pressure (middle), and temperature (bottom) wires on the engine

7. Remove the grille, the inner trim mounting bolts, and the lower radiator trim panel.

8. Loosen the lower radiator mounting bolt and unscrew the heat sensing switch carefully.

9. Remove the radiator drain plug and let the antifreeze drain into a suitable

container for reuse later when refilling the radiator. When the coolant has drained, remove the lower radiator hose.

10. Loosen the mounting bar and slide the upper radiator trim panel to the center of the car to disconnect it. Remove the upper radiator mountings and disconnect the upper radiator hose.

11. Disconnect the wire from the radiator blower motor, remove the hose from the intake manifold and heater, loosen the radiator side mounting bolt, and remove the radiator and fan motor; raise the front of the car and safely support it.

12. Disconnect the exhaust pipe at the manifold and loosen the transmission mounting bracket.

13. Remove the front engine mount. Loosen the mounting bolt at the engine block and disconnect the three starter wires; remove the starter assembly.

14. Remove all transmission to engine mounting bolts and flywheel guard (manual transmission) or torque converter guard (automatic transmission).

15. If the car is equipped with an automatic transmission, remove the three torque converter to flywheel bolts by working through the starter hole. A bar or strong screwdriver should be used to hold the flywheel while removing the bolts. Lower the car so that the weight is now on the wheels.

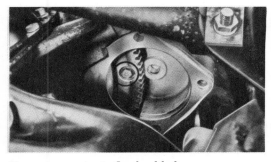

Torque converter-to-flywheel bolt

16. Pull the vacuum hose through the eye at the left rear of the cylinder head.

17. Attach a hoist and chain to the lifting points of the engine and lift the engine slightly to remove the right and left side engine mounts.

18. With this done, lower the hoist so that the wheels are supporting the weight of the car again.

19. With the automatic transmission,

Vacuum hose at the left rear of the cylinder head

Lifting the engine with a chain hoist

Special tool installed to prevent torque converter from falling out

support the transmission with a suitable jack (a transmission jack that will give proper support in the necessary areas); remove the transmission from the engine carefully and lift the engine straight out. When the engine has been separated from the transmission, use special tool 32-200 or a suitable bar to prevent the torque converter from falling out.

20. On cars equipped with a manual transmission, after the engine mounts have been removed and the car is on the ground, pry the engine and transmission apart and remove the intermediate plate from the engine. Lift out the engine while turning it to obtain enough clearance.

Installation

21. Installation is the reverse of removal, but note the following precautions:

a. Make sure that the intermediate plate is on the positioning pins; it can be held in place on the engine with a liberal application of grease;

b. The engine must be lowered carefully into the engine compartment to avoid component damage;

c. Use a transmission jack to properly align the mainshaft for the transmission with the engine to avoid damaging the shaft;

d. On cars with an automatic transmission, use new torque converter bolts when connecting it to the flywheel.

FOX WITH AIR CONDITIONING (REMOVING ENGINE AND TRANSMISSION TOGETHER)

On air conditioned models of the Fox, it is necessary to lower the engine, transmission, and front suspension from the car as a unit.

1. Raise the car, allowing the front wheels to hang down. Disconnect the battery.

2. Drain the battery.

3. Remove all the connections between the engine, transmission and body as described in the previous section.

4. Remove the radiator and the gearshift rod coupling at the transmission.

5. Remove the front engine mount at the engine block.

6. Use a puller to separate the tie-rod ends from the steering levers.

Removing the tie-rod ends with a puller (Tool 40-14)

7. Push the brake pedal down about 1½ in. and fasten it in place to keep the system from draining. Disconnect and plug the brake lines at the brackets on the wheel housing.

8. Attach a framework to the engine to keep the assembly steady and support it from underneath with a floor jack clamped to the crossmember. Lift the unit slightly and disconnect both coil springs from the wheel housings; unbolt the crossmember.

9. If the car is equipped with an automatic transmission, remove the transmission support bracket, detach the selector lever cable from the transmission, and pull off the kickdown switch wire.

Back-up switch wire (arrow)

10. Disconnect the backup light switch wire and lower the engine, transmission, and front suspension assembly.

11. Installation is the reverse of removal; tighten the coil spring units to the body to 16 ft lbs., and the crossmember to the body to 33 ft lbs.

Engine Mounting Torques (ft lbs)

Torque converter bolts—25
Engine-to-transmission—40
Left and right engine mounts—32
Front engine mounts—18

TIMING BELT COVER

Removal and Installation

1. Loosen the alternator mounting bolts.

2. Pivot the alternator over and slip the drive belt off the pulleys.

3. Unscrew the cover retaining nuts and remove the cover. Don't lose any of the washers or spacers.

4. Reposition the spacers on the studs and then install the washers and nuts.

5. Install the alternator belt and tension as described earlier in this chapter.

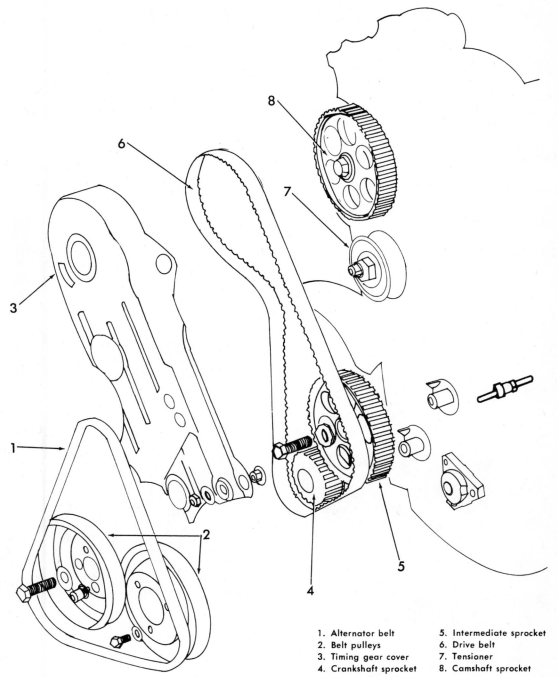

Exploded view of timing belt assembly

1. Alternator belt
2. Belt pulleys
3. Timing gear cover
4. Crankshaft sprocket
5. Intermediate sprocket
6. Drive belt
7. Tensioner
8. Camshaft sprocket

TIMING BELT

The timing belt and timing gears drive the camshaft at ½ the crankshaft speed. As the crankshaft rotates, it turns the crankshaft gear which in turn powers the timing belt. The belt runs to the top of the engine where it goes around the camshaft gear. When turning the camshaft gear, it also turns the camshaft, which acts on the tappets opening and closing the valves to let the gas/air mixture into the cylinder area and expel the exhaust gases when the combustion process is over.

NOTE: *The Fox timing belt is designed to last for more than 60,000 miles and does not normally require tension adjustments. If the belt is removed or replaced, the basic valve timing must be checked and the belt retensioned.*

Removal, Installation, and Tensioning

1. Remove the timing belt cover as previously outlined.

2. While holding the large hex on the tension pulley, loosen the pulley locknut.

3. Release the tensioner from the timing belt.

4. Slide the belt off the three toothed pulleys and remove it.

5. Turn the crankshaft sprocket with a socket wrench until the TDC mark aligns with the pointer in the transmission case opening. At the same time, the rotor in the distributor must align with the notch in the distributor housing.

6. Check that the timing punch mark on the rear of the camshaft sprocket is aligned with the cylinder head cover gasket. If it does not, turn the camshaft sprocket until it does.

The punchmark on the camshaft sprocket aligned with the notch on the cylinder head gasket for timing belt installation

7. Check that the intermediate sprocket punch mark is aligned with the notch on the crankshaft pulley. If they do not align, turn the crankshaft sprocket until they do.

CAUTION: *If the timing marks are not correctly aligned with the No. 1 piston at TDC of the compression stroke and the belt is installed, valve*

Intermediate sprocket mark aligned with the notch on the crankshaft pulley

timing will be incorrect. Poor performance and possible engine damage can result from improper valve timing.

8. To make the installation of the timing belt easier, remove the water pump pulley before attempting to install the belt.

Releasing the tensioner. Turn in direction (a) to tension the belt and (b) to release tension. Check tension at midpoint (c)

9. With the belt on, adjust tensioner by turning the large tensioner hex nut to the right. Tension is correct when you can twist the belt 90° (sideways) with two fingers at the midpoint between the camshaft pulley and the intermediate shaft sprocket. Tighten the locknut to 32 ft lbs.

10. Install the timing belt cover and check the ignition timing as described in Chapter 2.

TIMING GEARS

Removal and Installation

The camshaft, intermediate shaft, and crankshaft pulleys are located by keys on their respective shafts and each is retained by a bolt. To remove any or all of the pulleys, first remove the timing belt cover and belt as outlined above and then use the following procedure.

NOTE: *When removing the crankshaft pulley, don't remove the four socket head bolts which retain the outer belt pulley to the timing belt pulley.*

1. Remove the center bolt.
2. Gently pry the pulley off the shaft.
3. If the pulley is stubborn in coming off, use a gear puller. Don't hammer on the pulley.
4. Remove the pulley and key.
5. Install the pulley in the reverse order of removal.
6. Tighten the center bolt to 58 ft lbs.
7. Install the timing belt, check valve timing, tension belt, and install the cover.

CAMSHAFT

The camshaft is a machined rod in the top of the Fox's engine with lobes which work with the tappets to open and close the valves. On the Fox, the camshaft is an overhead type, which means that it is positioned above the valves and acts directly on them, instead of using pushrods and rocker arms. The camshaft has two lobes for each cylinder and is driven by the timing belt. These lobes turn around, pushing down on tappets which open and close the valves of that particular cylinder. The cam lobe will first push down on the intake valve opening it to allow the air/fuel mixture to enter the cylinder area, then close the intake valve to seal the area for the combustion process. After the combustion process, the cam lobe for the exhaust valve will force down on it, opening it to expel the exhaust gasses and then closing it to seal it for the next combustion cycle.

Removal and Installation

1. Remove the timing belt.
2. Remove the camshaft sprocket.
3. Remove the air cleaner.
4. Remove the camshaft cover.
5. Unscrew and remove the Nos. 1, 3,

and 5 bearing caps (No. 1 is at front of engine).

6. Unscrew the Nos. 2 and 4 bearing caps, diagonally and in increments. Be very careful during this step to release the pressure on the caps evenly so that the spring pressure will not damage the camshaft.
7. Lift the camshaft out of the cylinder head.
8. Lubricate the camshaft journals and lobes with assembly lube or gear oil before installing it in the cylinder head.
9. Replace the camshaft oil seal with a new one whenever the cam is removed.
10. Install the No. 5 bearing cap first since it serves as a guide for the camshaft, then proceed to install Nos. 1 and 3, tightening the nuts on all three to 14 ft lbs. The caps should be installed so that the numbers can be read, right side up, from the drivers seat.
11. Install the Nos. 2 and 4 bearing caps and diagonally tighten the nuts to 14 ft lbs.

NOTE: *If checking end-play, install a dial indicator so that the feeler touches the camshaft tip. End-play should be no more than 0.006 in. (0.15 mm).*

12. Replace the seal in the No. 1 bearing cap. If necessary, replace the end plug in the cylinder head.
13. Install the camshaft cover.
14. Install the camshaft pulley and the timing belt as previously described.
15. Check the valve clearance as outlined in Chapter 2.

NOTE: *The manufacturer advises that the camshaft must not be removed unless a special removal tool is used. This device bolts to the cylinder head and pressed down on the camshaft at two places: between the lobes for cylinder 3 and between the lobes for cylinder 2. The preceding alternate procedure may be used, but great caution must be used. The alternate procedure is not recommended by the manufacturer.*

CYLINDER HEAD

The cylinder head is that area in which the valves lie in the Fox. Its function is to seal the top of the block so that the combustion process can occur. It lies directly on top of the block and has the intake and exhaust manifolds connected to it. These, in conjunction with the valves, let the fuel air mixture into and out of the block as the combustion cycle is completed.

Removal and Installation

The engine should be cold before the cylinder head can be removed. The head is retained by 10 socket head bolts. It can be removed without removing the intake and exhaust manifolds.

1. Disconnect the battery ground cable.
2. Drain the cooling system.
3. Remove the air cleaner. Disconnect the fuel line.
4. Disconnect the radiator, heater, and choke hoses.
5. Disconnect all electrical wires. Remove the spark plug wires.
6. Separate the exhaust manifold from the exhaust pipe.
7. Disconnect the EGR line from the exhaust manifold. Remove the EGR valve and filter from the intake manifold.
8. Remove the carburetor; disconnect the accelerator cable from the mounting bracket on the intake manifold.
9. On cars so equipped, disconnect the air pump fittings.
10. Remove the timing belt cover and belt, and the alternator belt.
11. Loosen the cylinder head bolts in the sequence of 10 to 1 as shown in the illustration.

Cylinder head tightening sequence

12. Remove the bolts and lift the cylinder head straight off.
13. Install the new cylinder head gasket with the word "top" (oben) going up.
14. Install bolts Nos. 7 and 8 first, these holes are smaller and will properly locate the gasket and cylinder head.
15. Install the remaining bolts. Tighten them in three stages in the 1 through 10 sequence shown. Cylinder head tightening torque is 55 ft lbs.

NOTE: *After approximately 300 miles, retighten these cylinder head bolts.*
16. Install the remaining components in the reverse order of removal.

Overhaul

The "Engine Rebuilding" section contains general information on cylinder head refinishing. This job is best left to a dealer or a competent machinist, as they will have the correct tools. Valve guides are a shrink fit. Always install new valve seals. Valve seats are not replaceable, the cylinder head should be replaced if the valve pocket depth exceeds 0.354 in. (9 mm) for intake valves and/or 0.378 in. (9.6 mm) for exhaust valves.

VALVE LASH

Valve lash in the Fox is the distance between the cam lobe and the adjusting disc. It is one factor that determines how far the intake and exhaust valves open into the cylinder. If there is too much valve lash, part of the lift of the camshaft will be used in removing the excess clearance, therefore the valves will not open far enough. This means that the necessary distance covered by the camshaft will be greater, so the net effect on the valves will be less. This has two ill effects; as the excess clearance is removed, the valve gear (valves, tappets, and cam lobes), will become noisier, and as the valves are opened improperly, the engine will perform poorly. This is because the intake valves will admit a smaller amount of the air-fuel mix into the cylinders, creating less of an explosion than is supposed to take place. Exhaust valves which aren't opening the full amount tend to create more backpressure in the cylinder which impedes the entry of the next fuel-air charge.

If the valve clearance is too small, the valves will not seat or position themselves on the cylinder head when they fully close. When a valve seats it does two things; it seals the combustion chamber so that none of the gases in the cylinder can escape and it cools itself by transferring some of the heat absorbed in the combustion process through the cylinder head and into the cooling system. Therefore if the valve clearance is too small, the gases will escape the combustion chamber and as a result, the engine

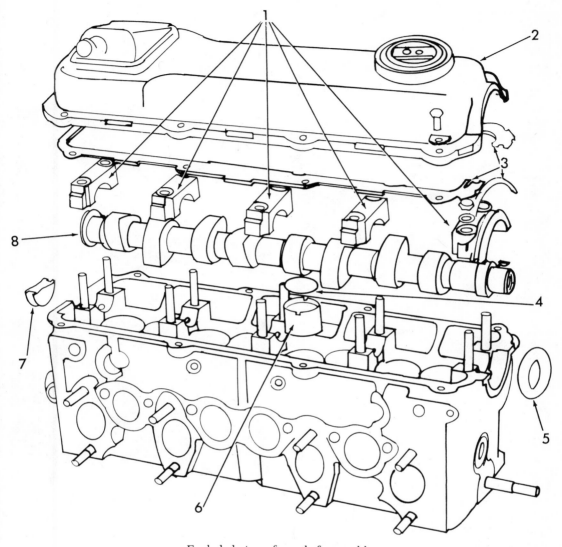

Exploded view of camshaft assembly

1. Camshaft bearing caps
2. Camshaft cover
3. Gasket
4. Valve adjusting disc
5. Oil seal
6. Cam follower
7. End plug
8. Camshaft

will run poorly. The valves will also overheat since they cannot properly transfer heat to the cooling system. While all valve adjustment must be as accurate as possible, it is better to have the adjustment slightly loose than tight, as burned valves can result from too tight an adjustment.

Adjustment

Audi recommends that you check the valve clearance at 1,000 miles and then at every 20,000 miles after that. The over-head cam in the Fox acts directly on the valves through tappets which fit over the valve springs and valves. Adjustment is made by replacing an adjustment disc which fits into the tappet. By varying the thickness of the discs, you can vary the valve lash. Valve clearance must be checked with the engine warmed up to normal operating temperatures.

When doing the following procedure, you should be aware that there are 26 different sizes of discs available for you to adjust the cam clearance with. It will be

Valve adjusting discs and adjusting tools

impossible for you to know beforehand exactly what size will be needed for your Fox. There are two possible ways to proceed in this situation, they are: check the clearance yourself, and if found to be excessive, take the car to a dealer and have him put the new discs in; or remove the discs from the tappets with too much clearance, check the size of the old discs and go to a dealer to pick up the proper size replacement. If you're going to follow the second suggestion, make sure that you make a note of which disc came from which valve so you don't run into trouble when you go to replace them.

1. Remove the air cleaner and hoses which attach to the camshaft cover. Also remove the spark plugs if you have not already done so.

2. Remove the eight bolts and lift off the camshaft cover.

3. Valve clearance is checked in the firing order, that is, check the valves of number 1 cylinder first, followed by Nos. 3, 4, and 2 with the piston of the cylinder being checked, at TDC of the compression stroke. TDC is the spot where both valves are closed and the plug is firing the mixture. Both cam lobes at TDC

should be pointing up. To obtain TDC for any cylinder, remove the front license plate (if equipped), and turn the crankshaft pulley nut with a socket wrench to position the camshaft for checking.

Turning the crankshaft over to bring a cylinder into position for checking the valve lash

Checking valve lash with a feeler gauge

4. With the No. 1 piston at TDC, determine the clearance with a feeler gauge. Intake clearance should be 0.008–0.012 in. (0.20–0.30 mm); exhaust clearance should be 0.016–0.020 in. (0.40–0.50 mm). You can determine which valves are intake and which are exhaust by referring to the accompanying illustration.

◄ **FRONT**   E I E I I E I E

Fox valve positions

E Exhaust valve   I Intake valve

5. Continue on to check the other three cylinders in the firing order (3, 4, and 2), turning the crankshaft to bring that piston to the top of the compression stroke (TDC). Record the valve clear-

ances on a piece of paper as you go along.

If adjustment is necessary, the disc(s) will have to be removed and replaced with thicker or thinner ones, whichever will yield the proper clearance. For the first adjustment, thinner discs will probably be needed. Discs are available in 0.002 in. (0.05 mm) increments from 0.12 in. (3.00 mm) to 0.17 in. (4.25 mm). The disc size is scribed into the underside of the disc; this side will always face the tappet.

Audi recommends that two special tools be used to remove and install the adjustment discs. One is a pry bar (VW tool 1-546) used to compress the valve springs and the other is a pair of special pliers (VW tool 10-208) used to grip and remove the adjustment disc.

Removing or installing the valve adjustment discs

A flat metal bar can be used to compress the spring if you take care not to damage the cam lobes. The tappet has two slots which permit the pliers to grasp the disc and lift it out, but here it's also possible to improvise with a thin blade screwdriver used to remove the disc. The best way to do this job is for an assistant to hold down the spring, leaving both your hands free to work the disc out.

6. Replace the adjustment discs as necessary to bring the clearance to within the 0.002 in. (0.05 mm) tolerance.

7. Recheck all valve clearances after adjustment, and replace the camshaft cover with a new gasket, and replace the air cleaner.

INTAKE MANIFOLD

The intake manifold takes the fuel-air mixture from the carburetor and delivers it to the valves where it enters the combustion chamber through the intake valve and is ignited.

Removal and Installation

1. Remove the air cleaner. Drain the cooling system.

2. Disconnect the accelerator cable.

3. Disconnect the EGR valve connections.

4. Detach all electrical leads.

5. Disconnect the coolant hoses.

6. Disconnect the fuel line from the carburetor.

7. Remove the vacuum hoses from the carburetor.

8. Loosen and remove the six retaining bolts and lift off the manifold.

9. Install a new gasket. Fit the manifold and tighten the bolts from the inside out. Tightening torque is 18 ft lbs.

10. Install the remaining components in the reverse order of removal. Refill the cooling system.

EXHAUST MANIFOLD

The exhaust manifold is connected between the cylinder head and the exhaust system, and serves to gather the burned exhaust gases and pass them through the exhaust system into the air.

1. Disconnect the EGR tube from the exhaust manifold.

2. On California cars, remove the air pump components which are in the way.

3. Remove the air cleaner hose from the exhaust manifold.

4. Disconnect the intake manifold support.

5. Separate the exhaust pipe from the manifold.

6. Remove the eight retaining nuts and remove the manifold.

7. Clean the cylinder head and manifold mating surfaces.

8. Using a new gasket, install the exhaust manifold.

9. Tighten the nuts to 18 ft lbs. Work from the inside out.

10. Install the remaining components in the reverse order of removal. Use a new manifold flange gasket if the old one is deteriorated.

PISTONS AND CONNECTING RODS

Removal and Installation

NOTE: *A complete step-by-step engine rebuilding section is included at the end of this chapter.*

1. Follow the instructions under "Cylinder Head Removal" and "Timing Belt Removal."

2. Remove the oil pan as described later in this chapter.

3. This procedure would be much more easily performed with the engine out of the car.

4. Pistons should be removed in the order: 1-3-4-2. Turn the crankshaft until the piston to be removed is at the bottom of its stroke.

5. Place a cloth on the head of the piston to be removed and, using a ridge reamer, remove the deposits from the upper end of the cylinder bore.

NOTE: *Never remove more than* 1/32 *in. from the ring travel area when removing the ridges.*

6. Mark all connecting rod bearing caps so that they may be returned to their original locations in the engine.

7. Remove the connecting rod caps.

8. Push the connecting rod and piston out through the top of the cylinder with a hammer handle.

CAUTION: *Don't score the cylinder walls or the crankshaft journal.*

9. Using an internal micrometer or a dial gauge, measure the bore of the cylinder as shown in the illustration. The measurements should be made in three places, 3/8 in. (10 mm) from the top and bottom of the cylinder and in the center of the cylinder. At each measurement location, two measurements should be taken, one from left-to-right, and the other from front-to-rear. The bore must not be out-of-round by more than 0.001 in. (0.03 mm). See the "Engine Rebuilding" section for complete details.

10. If the cylinder bore is in satisfactory condition, place each ring in the bore in turn and push it in the bore with the head of the piston. Measure the ring gap. If the ring gap is greater than the limit, get a new ring. If the ring gap is less than the limit, file the end of the ring to obtain the correct gap.

11. Check the ring side clearance by installing rings on the piston, and inserting a feeler gauge of the correct dimension between the ring and the lower land. The gauge should slide freely around the ring circumference without binding. Any wear will form a step on the lower edge. Remove any pistons having high steps.

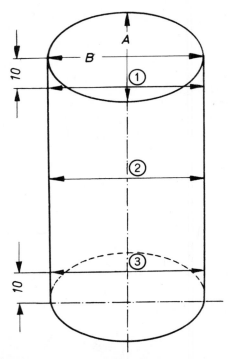

Cylinder measurement locations

1. Take bore measurements in directions "A" and "B," at this point, 3/8 in. (10 mm) from the top.
2. Take bore measurements in directions "A" and "B," at this point, in the center of the cylinder.
3. Take bore measurements in directions "A" and "B," at ths point, 3/8 in. (10 mm) from the bottom of the cylinder.

Before checking the ring side clearance, be sure that the ring grooves are clean and free of carbon, sludge, or grit.

12. Piston rings should be installed so that their ends are at three equal spacings, i.e., the openings are 120° apart. Do not install the rings with their ends in line with the piston pin bosses (notch) and the thrust direction.

13. Install the pistons in their original bores, if you are reusing the same pistons. Install short lengths of rubber hose over the connecting rod bolts to prevent damage to the cylinder walls or rod journal. When replacing the pistons, make sure that new connecting rod bolts are used.

14. Install a ring compressor over the rings on the piston. Lower the piston and rod assembly into the bore until the ring compressor contacts the block. Using a wooden handle, push the piston into the bore while guiding the rod onto the journal.

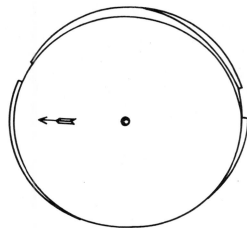

Arrow on piston must face forward

NOTE: *The arrow on the piston should face toward the front of the engine.*

ENGINE REBUILDING NOTES

Use the "Engine Rebuilding" section at the end of the chapter for cylinder head, block, and crankshaft refinishing. The main bearing shells with the lubricating grooves always go in the block, not the caps, for proper oiling. There is a piston size code stamped on the cylinder block above the water pump. Bring this number to the dealer when ordering a replacement pistons(s).

Engine Lubrication

The Fox lubrication system is of conventional wet-sump design. The gear type oil pump is driven by the intermediate shaft. A pressure relief valve limits pressure and prevents extreme pressure from developing in the system. All oil is filtered by a full-flow replaceable filter. A by-pass valve assures lubrication in the event that the filter becomes plugged. The oil pressure switch is located at the end of the cylinder head galley (the end of the system) to assure accurate pressure readings.

OIL PAN

Removal and Installation

The front crossmember has to be lowered to remove the oil pan.

1. Raise the car, allowing the front wheels to hang down, and drain the oil.

2. On cars with automatic transmissions, disconnect the engine vacuum line from the power brake vacuum line T fitting, and pull the line from the cylinder head.

3. Slightly raise the rear of the engine with an overhead hoist connected to the lifting eye cast in the rear of the cylinder head.

4. Remove the flywheel guard plate.

5. From underneath, unbolt the left and right engine mounts. Carefully and evenly, loosen and remove the four crossmember-to-body bolts and lower the crossmember.

Engine mount locations

6. Remove the pan bolts; tap the pan with a soft hammer to break it loose. Remove the pan and clean it thoroughly while it is off the engine.

7. To install, use a new gasket but NO sealer. Torque the pan bolts in a crisscross pattern, in steps, to 6 ft lbs.

8. Raise the crossmember into position and tighten the crossmember bolts to 33 ft lbs. Tighten the engine mounting bolts to 30 ft lbs and replace the flywheel guard plate.

REAR MAIN OIL SEAL

Replacement

The rear main oil seal is located in a housing on the rear of the cylinder block. To replace the seal, it is necessary to remove the transmission and perform the work from underneath the car or remove the engine and perform the work on an engine stand or work bench. See Chapter 6 for "Transmission Removal and Installation."

1. Remove the transmission and flywheel.

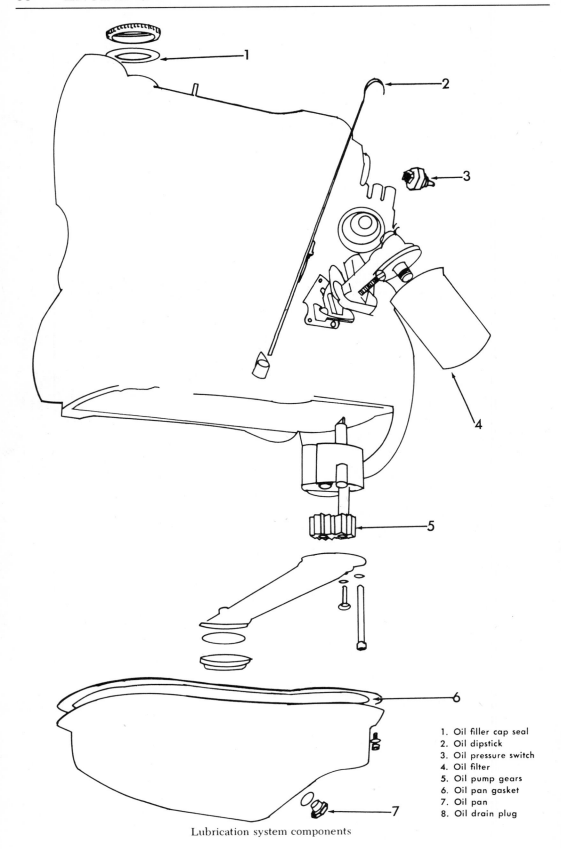

1. Oil filler cap seal
2. Oil dipstick
3. Oil pressure switch
4. Oil filter
5. Oil pump gears
6. Oil pan gasket
7. Oil pan
8. Oil drain plug

Lubrication system components

Removing the old oil seal from the support ring

2. Using a screwdriver, very carefully pry the old seal out of the support ring.

3. Remove the seal.

4. Lightly oil the replacement seal and then press it into place using a canister top or other circular piece of flat metal. Be careful not to damage the seal or score the crankshaft.

5. Press the seal on to its limit with special tool 10-220, by tightening the flywheel mounting bolts alternately to 46 ft lbs.

Using a special tool to press in the new seal

6. Remove the tool and install the flywheel and transmission, torquing the bolts to 46 ft lbs.

OIL PUMP

The oil pump is driven by the distributor shaft which is in turn driven by the intermediate crankshaft sprocket. It picks up oil from the pan and distributes it throughout the engine to remove heat and lubricate the internal components of the engine.

Removal and Installation

1. Remove the oil pan.
2. Remove the two mounting bolts.
3. Pull oil pump down and out of the engine.

4. Unscrew the two bolts and separate the pump halves.
5. Remove the driveshaft and gear from the upper body.
6. Clean the bottom half in solvent. Pry up the metal edges to remove the filter screen for cleaning.
7. Examine the gears and driveshaft for wear or damage. Replace them if necessary.
8. Reassemble the pump halves.
9. Prime the pump with oil and install in the reverse order of removal.

Engine Cooling

The Fox cooling system consists of a belt-driven, external water pump, thermostat, radiator, and thermo-switch controlled electric cooling fan. When the engine is cold the thermostat is closed and blocks the water from the radiator so that the coolant is only circulated through the engine. When the engine warms up, the thermostat opens and the radiatior is included in the coolant circuit. The thermo-switch is positioned in the bottom of the radiator and turns the electrical fan on at 199°F, off at 189°F. This reduces power loss and engine noise.

RADIATOR AND FAN

Removal and Installation

1. Remove the radiator grille.
2. Remove the inner trim mounting bolts; remove the lower radiator trim panel.
3. Loosen the lower radiator mounting nut, drain the coolant, and remove the lower radiator hose.
4. Disconnect the thermoswitch.
5. After loosening the upper mounting bar, slide the upper radiator trim panel to the center of the car and disconnect it. Remove all the radiator mountings and disconnect the upper radiator hose.
6. Disconnect the wire from the blower motor; and remove the hoses from the intake manifold and heater.
7. Loosen the radiator side mounting bolt and remove the radiator and fan.

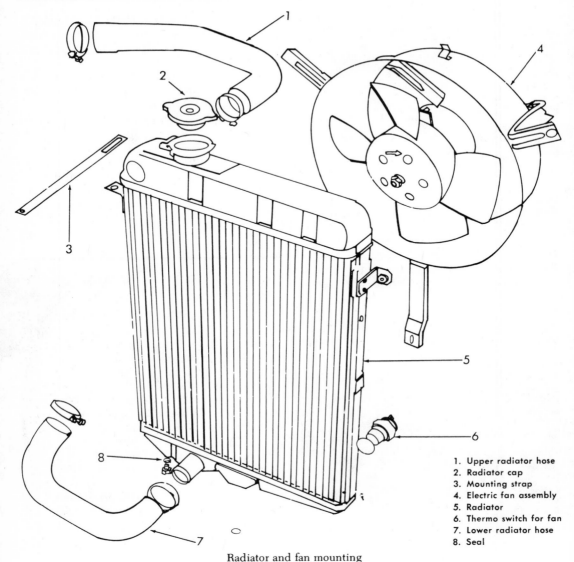

Radiator and fan mounting

1. Upper radiator hose
2. Radiator cap
3. Mounting strap
4. Electric fan assembly
5. Radiator
6. Thermo switch for fan
7. Lower radiator hose
8. Seal

THERMOSTAT

Removal and Installation

The thermostat is located in the bottom radiator hose neck on the water pump.

1. Drain the cooling system.

2. Remove the two retaining bolts from the lower water pump neck.

NOTE: *It's not necessary to disconnect the hose.*

3. Move the neck, with hoses attached, out of the way.

4. Remove the thermostat.

5. Install a new seal on the water pump neck.

6. Install the thermostat with the spring end up.

7. Replace the water pump neck and tighten the two retaining bolts.

WATER PUMP

The water pump, powered by the fan belt, forces water through the engine to cool the system. The pump's impeller a vaned wheel inside the pump housing, traps water between the vanes of the wheel. This trapped water forces the wheel to rotate and the resulting centrifugal force raises the pressure in the pump causing water to flow through it and into the engine under pressure. After the water has been through the engine, it returns to the radiator where it is cooled down by the passage of air through the fins and then drawn back into the engine by the pump.

Removal and Installation

1. Drain the cooling system.
2. Remove the alternator and drive belt as outlined earlier in this chapter.

3. Remove the timing belt cover.
4. Disconnect the lower radiator hose, engine hose, and heater hose from the water pump.
5. Remove the four pump retaining bolts. Notice where the different length bolts are located.
6. Turn the pump slightly and lift it out of the engine block.
7. Installation is the reverse of removal. Use a new seal on the mating surface of the engine.

Engine Rebuilding

This section describes, in detail, the procedures involved in rebuilding a typical engine. The procedures specifically refer to an inline engine, however, they are basically identical to those used in rebuilding engines of nearly all design and configurations. Procedures for servicing atypical engines (i.e., horizontally opposed) are described in the appropriate section, although in most cases, cylinder head reconditioning procedures described in this chapter will apply.

The section is divided into two sections. The first, Cylinder Head Reconditioning, assumes that the cylinder head is removed from the engine, all manifolds are removed, and the cylinder head is on a workbench. The camshaft should be removed from overhead cam cylinder heads. The second section, Cylinder Block Reconditioning, covers the block, pistons, connecting rods and crankshaft. It is assumed that the engine is mounted on a work stand, and the cylinder head and all accessories are removed.

Procedures are identified as follows:

Unmarked—Basic procedures that must be performed in order to successfully complete the rebuilding process.

Starred (*)—Procedures that should be performed to ensure maximum performance and engine life.

Double starred (**)—Procedures that may be performed to increase engine performance and reliability. These procedures are usually reserved for extremely heavy-duty or competition usage.

In many cases, a choice of methods is also provided. Methods are identified in the same manner as procedures. The choice of method for a procedure is at the discretion of the user.

The tools required for the basic rebuilding procedure should, with minor exceptions, be those

TORQUE (ft. lbs.) *

U.S.

Bolt Diameter (inches)	Bolt Grade (SAE)				Wrench Size (inches)	
	1 and 2	5	6	8	Bolt	Nut
1/4	5	7	10	10.5	3/8	7/16
5/16	9	14	19	22	1/2	9/16
3/8	15	25	34	37	9/16	5/8
7/16	24	40	55	60	5/8	3/4
1/2	37	60	85	92	3/4	13/16
9/16	53	88	120	132	7/8	7/8
5/8	74	120	167	180	15/16	1
3/4	120	200	280	296	1-1/8	1-1/8
7/8	190	302	440	473	1-5/16	1-5/16
1	282	466	660	714	1-1/2	1-1/2

Metric

Bolt Diameter (mm)	Bolt Grade				Wrench Size (mm)
	5D	8G	10K	12K	Bolt and Nut
6	5	6	8	10	10
8	10	16	22	27	14
10	19	31	40	49	17
12	34	54	70	86	19
14	55	89	117	137	22
16	83	132	175	208	24
18	111	182	236	283	27
22	182	284	394	464	32
24	261	419	570	689	36

*—Torque values are for lightly oiled bolts. CAUTION: Bolts threaded into aluminum require much less torque.

General Torque Specifications

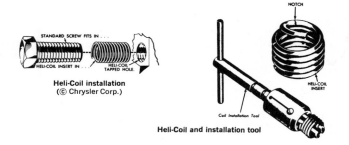

Heli-Coil installation
(© Chrysler Corp.)

Heli-Coil and installation tool

Heli-Coil Insert			Drill	Tap	Insert. Tool	Extracting Tool
Thread Size	Part No.	Insert Length (In.)	Size		Part No.	Part No.
1/2 -20	1185-4	3/8	17/64(.266)	4 CPB	528-4N	1227-6
5/16-18	1185-5	15/32	Q(.332)	5 CPB	528-5N	1227-6
3/8 -16	1185-6	9/16	X(.397)	6 CPB	528-6N	1227-6
7/16-14	1185-7	21/32	29/64(.453)	7 CPB	528-7N	1227-16
1/2 -13	1185-8	3/4	33/64(.516)	8 CPB	528-8N	1227-16

Heli-Coil Specifications

included in a mechanic's tool kit. An accurate torque wrench, and a dial indicator (reading in thousandths) mounted on a universal base should be available. Bolts and nuts with no torque specification should be tightened according to size (see chart). Special tools, where required, all are readily available from the major tool suppliers (i.e., Craftsman, Snap-On, K-D). The services of a competent automotive machine shop must also be readily available.

When assembling the engine, any parts that will be in frictional contact must be pre-lubricated, to provide protection on initial start-up. Vortex Pre-Lube, STP, or any product specifically formulated for this purpose may be used. NOTE: *Do not use engine oil.* Where semi-permanent (locked but removable) installation of bolts or nuts is desired, threads should be cleaned and coated with Loctite. Studs may be permanently installed using Loctite Stud and Bearing Mount.

Aluminum has become increasingly popular for use in engines, due to its low weight and excellent heat transfer characteristics. The following precautions

must be observed when handling aluminum engine parts:
—Never hot-tank aluminum parts.
—Remove all aluminum parts (identification tags, etc.) from engine parts before hot-tanking (otherwise they will be removed during the process).
—Always coat threads lightly with engine oil or anti-seize compounds before installation, to prevent seizure.
—Never over-torque bolts or spark plugs in aluminum threads. Should stripping occur, threads can be restored according to the following procedure, using Heli-Coil thread inserts:

Tap drill the hole with the stripped threads to the specified size (see chart). Using the specified tap (NOTE: *Heli-Coil tap sizes refer to the size thread being replaced, rather than the actual tap size*), tap the hole for the Heli-Coil. Place the insert on the proper installation tool (see chart). Apply pressure on the insert while winding it clockwise into the hole, until the top of the insert is one turn below the surface. Remove the installation tool, and break the installation tang from the bottom of the in-

sert by moving it up and down. If the Heli-Coil must be removed, tap the removal tool firmly into the hole, so that it engages the top thread, and turn the tool counter-clockwise to extract the insert.

Snapped bolts or studs may be removed, using a stud extractor (unthreaded) or Vise-Grip pliers (threaded). Penetrating oil (e.g., Liquid Wrench) will often aid in breaking frozen threads. In cases where the stud or bolt is flush with, or below the surface, proceed as follows:

Drill a hole in the broken stud or bolt, approximately ½ its diameter. Select a screw extractor (e.g., Easy-Out) of the proper size, and tap it into the stud or bolt. Turn the extractor counterclockwise to remove the stud or bolt.

Magnaflux and Zyglo are inspection techniques used to locate material flaws, such as stress cracks. Magnafluxing coats the part with fine magnetic particles, and subjects the part to a magnetic field. Cracks cause breaks

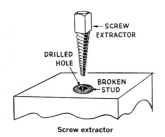

Screw extractor

in the magnetic field, which are outlined by the particles. Since Magnaflux is a magnetic process, it is applicable only to ferrous materials. The Zyglo process coats the material with a fluorescent dye penetrant, and then subjects it to blacklight inspection, under which cracks glow bright-

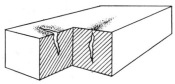

Magnaflux indication of cracks

ly. Parts made of any material may be tested using Zyglo. While Magnaflux and Zyglo are excellent for general inspection, and locating hidden defects, specific checks of suspected cracks may be made at lower cost and more readily using spot check dye. The dye is sprayed onto the suspected area, wiped off, and the area is then sprayed with a developer. Cracks then will show up brightly. Spot check dyes will only indicate surface cracks; therefore, structural cracks below the surface may escape detection. When questionable, the part should be tested using Magnaflux or Zyglo.

CYLINDER HEAD RECONDITIONING

Procedure	Method
Identify the valves:	Invert the cylinder head, and number the valve faces front to rear, using a permanent felt-tip marker.
Remove the rocker arms:	Remove the rocker arms with shaft(s) or balls and nuts. Wire the sets of rockers, balls and nuts together, and identify according to the corresponding valve.
Remove the valves and springs:	Using an appropriate valve spring compressor (depending on the configuration of the cylinder head), compress the valve springs. Lift out the keepers with needlenose pliers, release the compressor, and remove the valve, spring, and spring retainer.
Check the valve stem-to-guide clearance:	Clean the valve stem with lacquer thinner or a similar solvent to remove all gum and varnish. Clean the valve guides using solvent and an expanding wire-type valve guide cleaner. Mount a dial indicator so that the stem is at 90° to the valve stem, as close to the valve guide as possible. Move the valve off its seat, and measure the valve guide-to-stem clearance by moving the stem back and forth to actuate the dial indicator. Measure the valve stems using a micrometer, and compare to specifications, to determine whether stem or guide wear is responsible for excessive clearance.
De-carbon the cylinder head and valves:	Chip carbon away from the valve heads, combustion chambers, and ports, using a chisel made of hardwood. Remove the remaining deposits with a stiff wire brush. NOTE: *Ensure that the deposits are actually removed, rather than burnished.*

Checking the valve stem-to-guide clearance
(© American Motors Corp.)

Valve identification
(© SAAB)

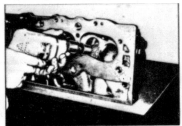

Removing carbon from the cylinder head
(© Chevrolet Div. G.M. Corp.)

Procedure	Method
Hot-tank the cylinder head:	Have the cylinder head hot-tanked to remove grease, corrosion, and scale from the water passages. NOTE: *In the case of overhead cam cylinder heads, consult the operator to determine whether the camshaft bearings will be damaged by the caustic solution.*
Degrease the remaining cylinder head parts:	Using solvent (i.e., Gunk), clean the rockers, rocker shaft(s) (where applicable), rocker balls and nuts, springs, spring retainers, and keepers. Do not remove the protective coating from the springs.
Check the cylinder head for warpage: Checking the cylinder head for warpage (© Ford Motor Co.)	Place a straight-edge across the gasket surface of the cylinder head. Using feeler gauges, determine the clearance at the center of the straight-edge. Measure across both diagonals, along the longitudinal centerline, and across the cylinder head at several points. If warpage exceeds .003″ in a 6″ span, or .006″ over the total length, the cylinder head must be resurfaced. NOTE: *If warpage exceeds the manufacturers maximum tolerance for material removal, the cylinder head must be replaced.* When milling the cylinder heads of V-type engines, the intake manifold mounting position is altered, and must be corrected by milling the manifold flange a proportionate amount.
** Porting and gasket matching:	** Coat the manifold flanges of the cylinder head with Prussian blue dye. Glue intake and exhaust gaskets to the cylinder head in their installed position using rubber cement and scribe the outline of the ports on the manifold flanges. Remove the gaskets. Using a small cutter in a hand-held power tool (i.e., Dremel Moto-Tool), gradually taper the walls of the port out to the scribed outline of the gasket. Further enlargement of the ports should include the removal of sharp edges and radiusing of sharp corners. Do not alter the valve guides. NOTE: *The most efficient port configuration is determined only by extensive testing. Therefore, it is best to consult someone experienced with the head in question to determine the optimum alterations.*

Checking the cylinder head for warpage
(© Ford Motor Co.)

(1)(3) CHECK DIAGONALLY
(2) CHECK ACROSS CENTER   A 2895-A

Marking the cylinder head for gasket matching
(© Petersen Publishing Co.)

Port configuration before and after gasket matching
(© Petersen Publishing Co.)

Procedure	*Method*

** Polish the ports:

Relieved and polished ports
(© Petersen Publishing Co.)

Polished combustion chamber
(© Petersen Publishing Co.)

** Using a grinding stone with the above mentioned tool, polish the walls of the intake and exhaust ports, and combustion chamber. Use progressively finer stones until all surface imperfections are removed. NOTE: *Through testing, it has been determined that a smooth surface is more effective than a mirror polished surface in intake ports, and vice-versa in exhaust ports.*

* Knurling the valve guides:

Cut-away view of a knurled valve guide
(© Petersen Publishing Co.)

* Valve guides which are not excessively worn or distorted may, in some cases, be knurled rather than replaced. Knurling is a process in which metal is displaced and raised, thereby reducing clearance. Knurling also provides excellent oil control. The possibility of knurling rather than replacing valve guides should be discussed with a machinist.

Replacing the valve guides: NOTE: *Valve guides should only be replaced if damaged or if an oversize valve stem is not available.*

A-VALVE GUIDE I.D.
B-SLIGHTLY SMALLER THAN VALVE GUIDE O.D.

Valve guide removal tool

WASHERS

A-VALVE GUIDE I.D.
B-LARGER THAN THE VALVE GUIDE O.D.

Valve guide installation tool (with washers used during installation)

Depending on the type of cylinder head, valve guides may be pressed, hammered, or shrunk in. In cases where the guides are shrunk into the head, replacement should be left to an equipped machine shop. In other cases, the guides are replaced as follows: Press or tap the valve guides out of the head using a stepped drift (see illustration). Determine the height above the boss that the guide must extend, and obtain a stack of washers, their I.D. similar to the guide's O.D., of that height. Place the stack of washers on the guide, and insert the guide into the boss. NOTE: *Valve guides are often tapered or beveled for installation.* Using the stepped installation tool (see illustration), press or tap the guides into position. Ream the guides according to the size of the valve stem.

Procedure	Method
Replacing valve seat inserts:	Replacement of valve seat inserts which are worn beyond resurfacing or broken, if feasible, must be done by a machine shop.
Resurfacing (grinding) the valve face:  **Grinding a valve** (ⓒ Subaru) 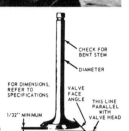 **Critical valve dimensions** (ⓒ Ford Motor Co.)	Using a valve grinder, resurface the valves according to specifications. CAUTION: *Valve face angle is not always identical to valve seat angle.* A minimum margin of 1/32″ should remain after grinding the valve. The valve stem tip should also be squared and resurfaced, by placing the stem in the V-block of the grinder, and turning it while pressing lightly against the grinding wheel.
Resurfacing the valve seats using reamers:  **Reaming the valve seat** (ⓒ S.p.A. Fiat) **Valve seat width and centering** (ⓒ Ford Motor Co.)	Select a reamer of the correct seat angle, slightly larger than the diameter of the valve seat, and assemble it with a pilot of the correct size. Install the pilot into the valve guide, and using steady pressure, turn the reamer clockwise. CAUTION: *Do not turn the reamer counter-clockwise.* Remove only as much material as necessary to clean the seat. Check the concentricity of the seat (see below). If the dye method is not used, coat the valve face with Prussian blue dye, install and rotate it on the valve seat. Using the dye marked area as a centering guide, center and narrow the valve seat to specifications with correction cutters. NOTE: *When no specifications are available, minimum seat width for exhaust valves should be 5/64″, intake valves 1/16″.* After making correction cuts, check the position of the valve seat on the valve face using Prussian blue dye.
* Resurfacing the valve seats using a grinder:  **Grinding a valve seat** (ⓒ Subaru)	Select a pilot of the correct size, and a coarse stone of the correct seat angle. Lubricate the pilot if necessary, and install the tool in the valve guide. Move the stone on and off the seat at approximately two cycles per second, until all flaws are removed from the seat. Install a fine stone, and finish the seat. Center and narrow the seat using correction stones, as described above.

Procedure	*Method*

Checking the valve seat concentricity:

Checking the valve seat concentricity using a dial gauge
(© American Motors Corp.)

Coat the valve face with Prussian blue dye, install the valve, and rotate it on the valve seat. If the entire seat becomes coated, and the valve is known to be concentric, the seat is concentric.

* Install the dial gauge pilot into the guide, and rest the arm on the valve seat. Zero the gauge, and rotate the arm around the seat. Run-out should not exceed .002″.

---

* Lapping the valves: NOTE: *Valve lapping is done to ensure efficient sealing of resurfaced valves and seats. Valve lapping alone is not recommended for use as a resurfacing procedure.*

Hand lapping the valves

HAND DRILL

ROD

SUCTION CUP

Home made mechanical valve lapping tool

* Invert the cylinder head, lightly lubricate the valve stems, and install the valves in the head as numbered. Coat valve seats with fine grinding compound, and attach the lapping tool suction cup to a valve head (NOTE: *Moisten the suction cup*). Rotate the tool between the palms, changing position and lifting the tool often to prevent grooving. Lap the valve until a smooth, polished seat is evident. Remove the valve and tool, and rinse away all traces of grinding compound.

** Fasten a suction cup to a piece of drill rod, and mount the rod in a hand drill. Proceed as above, using the hand drill as a lapping tool. CAUTION: *Due to the higher speeds involved when using the hand drill, care must be exercised to avoid grooving the seat.* Lift the tool and change direction of rotation often.

Check the valve springs:

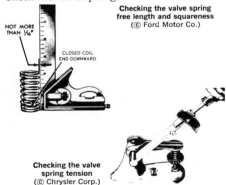

Checking the valve spring free length and squareness
(© Ford Motor Co.)

NOT MORE THAN 1/16″

CLOSED COIL END DOWNWARD

Checking the valve spring tension
(© Chrysler Corp.)

Place the spring on a flat surface next to a square. Measure the height of the spring, and rotate it against the edge of the square to measure distortion. If spring height varies (by comparison) by more than 1/16″ or if distortion exceeds 1/16″, replace the spring.

** In addition to evaluating the spring as above, test the spring pressure at the installed and compressed (installed height minus valve lift) height using a valve spring tester. Springs used on small displacement engines (up to 3 liters) should be ± 1 lb. of all other springs in either position. A tolerance of ± 5 lbs. is permissible on larger engines.

Procedure	Method
* Install valve stem seals:  **Valve stem seal installation** (© Ford Motor Co.) SEAL	* Due to the pressure differential that exists at the ends of the intake valve guides (atmospheric pressure above, manifold vacuum below), oil is drawn through the valve guides into the intake port. This has been alleviated somewhat since the addition of positive crankcase ventilation, which lowers the pressure above the guides. Several types of valve stem seals are available to reduce blow-by. Certain seals simply slip over the stem and guide boss, while others require that the boss be machined. Recently, Teflon guide seals have become popular. Consult a parts supplier or machinist concerning availability and suggested usages. NOTE: *When installing seals, ensure that a small amount of oil is able to pass the seal to lubricate the valve guides; otherwise, excessive wear may result.*
Install the valves:	Lubricate the valve stems, and install the valves in the cylinder head as numbered. Lubricate and position the seals (if used, see above) and the valve springs. Install the spring retainers, compress the springs, and insert the keys using needlenose pliers or a tool designed for this purpose. NOTE: *Retain the keys with wheel bearing grease during installation.*
Checking valve spring installed height: 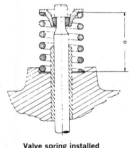 **Valve spring installed height dimension** (© Porsche) **Measuring valve spring installed height** (© Petersen Publishing Co.)	Measure the distance between the spring pad and the lower edge of the spring retainer, and compare to specifications. If the installed height is incorrect, add shim washers between the spring pad and the spring. CAUTION: *Use only washers designed for this purpose.*
** CC'ing the combustion chambers:	** Invert the cylinder head and place a bead of sealer around a combustion chamber. Install an apparatus designed for this purpose (burette mounted on a clear plate; see illustration) over the combustion chamber, and fill with the specified fluid to an even mark on the burette. Record the burette reading, and fill the combustion chamber with fluid. (NOTE: *A hole drilled in the plate will permit air to escape*). Subtract the burette reading, with the combustion chamber filled, from the previous reading, to determine combustion chamber volume in cc's. Duplicate this procedure in all combustion

Procedure	Method

CC'ing the combustion chamber (© Petersen Publishing Co.)

chambers on the cylinder head, and compare the readings. The volume of all combustion chambers should be made equal to that of the largest. Combustion chamber volume may be increased in two ways. When only a small change is required (usually), a small cutter or coarse stone may be used to remove material from the combustion chamber. NOTE: *Check volume frequently.* Remove material over a wide area, so as not to change the configuration of the combustion chamber. When a larger change is required, the valve seat may be sunk (lowered into the head). NOTE: *When altering valve seat, remember to compensate for the change in spring installed height.*

Inspect the rocker arms, balls, studs, and nuts (where applicable):

Stress cracks in rocker nuts (© Ford Motor Co.)

Visually inspect the rocker arms, balls, studs, and nuts for cracks, galling, burning, scoring, or wear. If all parts are intact, liberally lubricate the rocker arms and balls, and install them on the cylinder head. If wear is noted on a rocker arm at the point of valve contact, grind it smooth and square, removing as little material as possible. Replace the rocker arm if excessively worn. If a rocker stud shows signs of wear, it must be replaced (see below). If a rocker nut shows stress cracks, replace it. If an exhaust ball is galled or burned, substitute the intake ball from the same cylinder (if it is intact), and install a new intake ball. NOTE: *Avoid using new rocker balls on exhaust valves.*

Replacing rocker studs:

Reaming the stud bore for oversize rocker studs (© Buick Div. G.M. Corp.)

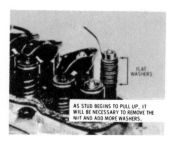

Extracting a pressed in rocker stud (© Buick Div. G.M. Corp.)

AS STUD BEGINS TO PULL UP, IT WILL BE NECESSARY TO REMOVE THE NUT AND ADD MORE WASHERS.

In order to remove a threaded stud, lock two nuts on the stud, and unscrew the stud using the lower nut. Coat the lower threads of the new stud with Loctite, and install.

Two alternative methods are available for replacing pressed in studs. Remove the damaged stud using a stack of washers and a nut (see illustration). In the first, the boss is reamed .005-.006″ oversize, and an oversize stud pressed in. Control the stud extension over the boss using washers, in the same manner as valve guides. Before installing the stud, coat it with white lead and grease. To retain the stud more positively, drill a hole through the stud and boss, and install a roll pin. In the second method, the boss is tapped, and a threaded stud installed. Retain the stud using Loctite Stud and Bearing Mount.

Procedure	*Method*
Inspect the rocker shaft(s) and rocker arms (where applicable):  **Disassembled rocker shaft parts arranged for inspection** (© American Motors Corp.) 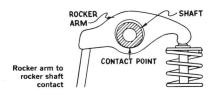 ROCKER ARM — SHAFT — CONTACT POINT — **Rocker arm to rocker shaft contact**	Remove rocker arms, springs and washers from rocker shaft. NOTE: *Lay out parts in the order they are removed.* Inspect rocker arms for pitting or wear on the valve contact point, or excessive bushing wear. Bushings need only be replaced if wear is excessive, because the rocker arm normally contacts the shaft at one point only. Grind the valve contact point of rocker arm smooth if necessary, removing as little material as possible. If excessive material must be removed to smooth and square the arm, it should be replaced. Clean out all oil holes and passages in rocker shaft. If shaft is grooved or worn, replace it. Lubricate and assemble the rocker shaft.
Inspect the camshaft bushings and the camshaft (overhead cam engines):	See next section.
Inspect the pushrods:	Remove the pushrods, and, if hollow, clean out the oil passages using fine wire. Roll each pushrod over a piece of clean glass. If a distinct clicking sound is heard as the pushrod rolls, the rod is bent, and must be replaced.
	* The length of all pushrods must be equal. Measure the length of the pushrods, compare to specifications, and replace as necessary.
Inspect the valve lifters:  Check for Concave Wear on Face of Tappet Using Tappet for Straight Edge **Checking the lifter face** (© American Motors Corp.)	Remove lifters from their bores, and remove gum and varnish, using solvent. Clean walls of lifter bores. Check lifters for concave wear as illustrated. If face is worn concave, replace lifter, and carefully inspect the camshaft. Lightly lubricate lifter and insert it into its bore. If play is excessive, an oversize lifter must be installed (where possible). Consult a machinist concerning feasibility. If play is satisfactory, remove, lubricate, and reinstall the lifter.
* Testing hydraulic lifter leak down: 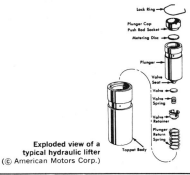 Lock Ring — Plunger Cap — Push Rod Socket — Metering Disc — Plunger — Valve Seat — Valve — Valve Spring — Valve Retainer — Plunger Return Spring — Tappet Body **Exploded view of a typical hydraulic lifter** (© American Motors Corp.)	Submerge lifter in a container of kerosene. Chuck a used pushrod or its equivalent into a drill press. Position container of kerosene so pushrod acts on the lifter plunger. Pump lifter with the drill press, until resistance increases. Pump several more times to bleed any air out of lifter. Apply very firm, constant pressure to the lifter, and observe rate at which fluid bleeds out of lifter. If the fluid bleeds very quickly (less than 15 seconds), lifter is defective. If the time exceeds 60 seconds, lifter is sticking. In either case, recondition or replace lifter. If lifter is operating properly (leak down time 15-60 seconds), lubricate and install it.

CYLINDER BLOCK RECONDITIONING

Procedure	*Method*
Checking the main bearing clearance:  **Plastigage installed on main bearing journal** (© Chevrolet Div. G.M. Corp.)  **Measuring Plastigage to determine main bearing clearance** (© Chevrolet Div. G.M. Corp.)  **Causes of bearing failure** (© Ford Motor Co.)	Invert engine, and remove cap from the bearing to be checked. Using a clean, dry rag, thoroughly clean all oil from crankshaft journal and bearing insert. NOTE: *Plastigage is soluble in oil; therefore, oil on the journal or bearing could result in erroneous readings.* Place a piece of Plastigage along the full length of journal, reinstall cap, and torque to specifications. Remove bearing cap, and determine bearing clearance by comparing width of Plastigage to the scale on Plastigage envelope. Journal taper is determined by comparing width of the Plastigage strip near its ends. Rotate crankshaft 90° and retest, to determine journal eccentricity. NOTE: *Do not rotate crankshaft with Plastigage installed.* If bearing insert and journal appear intact, and are within tolerances, no further main bearing service is required. If bearing or journal appear defective, cause of failure should be determined before replacement. * Remove crankshaft from block (see below). Measure the main bearing journals at each end twice (90° apart) using a micrometer, to determine diameter, journal taper and eccentricity. If journals are within tolerances, reinstall bearing caps at their specified torque. Using a telescope gauge and micrometer, measure bearing I.D. parallel to piston axis and at 30° on each side of piston axis. Subtract journal O.D. from bearing I.D. to determine oil clearance. If crankshaft journals appear defective, or do not meet tolerances, there is no need to measure bearings; for the crankshaft will require grinding and/or undersize bearings will be required. If bearing appears defective, cause for failure should be determined prior to replacement.
Checking the connecting rod bearing clearance:  **Plastigage installed on connecting rod bearing journal** (© Chevrolet Div. G.M. Corp.)	Connecting rod bearing clearance is checked in the same manner as main bearing clearance, using Plastigage. Before removing the crankshaft, connecting rod side clearance also should be measured and recorded. * Checking connecting rod bearing clearance, using a micrometer, is identical to checking main bearing clearance. If no other service

In the "Causes of bearing failure" figure:
SCRATCHES — SCRATCHED BY DIRT; DIRT IMBEDDED INTO BEARING MATERIAL; OVERLAY WIPED OUT — LACK OF OIL; BRIGHT (POLISHED) SECTIONS — IMPROPER SEATING; OVERLAY GONE FROM ENTIRE SURFACE — TAPERED JOURNAL; RADIUS RIDE — RADIUS RIDE; CRATERS OR POCKETS — FATIGUE FAILURE

Procedure	Method

**Measuring Plastigage to determine
connecting rod bearing clearance**
(© Chevrolet Div. G.M. Corp.)

is required, the piston and rod assemblies need not be removed.

Removing the crankshaft:

Connecting rod matching marks
(© Ford Motor Co.)

Using a punch, mark the corresponding main bearing caps and saddles according to position (i.e., one punch on the front main cap and saddle, two on the second, three on the third, etc.). Using number stamps, identify the corresponding connecting rods and caps, according to cylinder (if no numbers are present). Remove the main and connecting rod caps, and place sleeves of plastic tubing over the connecting rod bolts, to protect the journals as the crankshaft is removed. Lift the crankshaft out of the block.

Remove the ridge from the top of the cylinder:

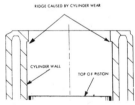

Cylinder bore ridge
(© Pontiac Div. G.M. Corp.)

In order to facilitate removal of the piston and connecting rod, the ridge at the top of the cylinder (unworn area; see illustration) must be removed. Place the piston at the bottom of the bore, and cover it with a rag. Cut the ridge away using a ridge reamer, exercising extreme care to avoid cutting too deeply. Remove the rag, and remove cuttings that remain on the piston. CAUTION: *If the ridge is not removed, and new rings are installed, damage to rings will result.*

Removing the piston and connecting rod:

Removing the piston
(© SAAB)

Invert the engine, and push the pistons and connecting rods out of the cylinders. If necessary, tap the connecting rod boss with a wooden hammer handle, to force the piston out. CAUTION: *Do not attempt to force the piston past the cylinder ridge* (see above).

Procedure	*Method*
Service the crankshaft:	Ensure that all oil holes and passages in the crankshaft are open and free of sludge. If necessary, have the crankshaft ground to the largest possible undersize.
	** Have the crankshaft Magnafluxed, to locate stress cracks. Consult a machinist concerning additional service procedures, such as surface hardening (e.g., nitriding, Tuftriding) to improve wear characteristics, cross drilling and chamfering the oil holes to improve lubrication, and balancing.
Removing freeze plugs:	Drill a hole in the center of the freeze plugs, and pry them out using a screwdriver or drift.
Remove the oil gallery plugs:	Threaded plugs should be removed using an appropriate (usually square) wrench. To remove soft, pressed in plugs, drill a hole in the plug, and thread in a sheet metal screw. Pull the plug out by the screw using pliers.
Hot-tank the block:	Have the block hot-tanked to remove grease, corrosion, and scale from the water jackets. NOTE: *Consult the operator to determine whether the camshaft bearings will be damaged during the hot-tank process.*
Check the block for cracks:	Visually inspect the block for cracks or chips. The most common locations are as follows: Adjacent to freeze plugs. Between the cylinders and water jackets. Adjacent to the main bearing saddles. At the extreme bottom of the cylinders. Check only suspected cracks using spot check dye (see introduction). If a crack is located, consult a machinist concerning possible repairs.
	** Magnaflux the block to locate hidden cracks. If cracks are located, consult a machinist about feasibility of repair.
Install the oil gallery plugs and freeze plugs:	Coat freeze plugs with sealer and tap into position using a piece of pipe, slightly smaller than the plug, as a driver. To ensure retention, stake the edges of the plugs. Coat threaded oil gallery plugs with sealer and install. Drive replacement soft plugs into block using a large drift as a driver.
	* Rather than reinstalling lead plugs, drill and tap the holes, and install threaded plugs.

Procedure	*Method*

Check the bore diameter and surface:

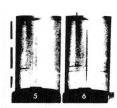

1, 2, 3 Piston skirt seizure resulted in this pattern. Engine must be rebored

4. Piston skirt and oil ring seizure caused this damage. Engine must be rebored

5, 6 Score marks caused by a split piston skirt. Damage is not serious enough to warrant reboring

7. Ring seized longitudinally, causing a score mark 1 3/16" wide, on the land side of the piston groove. The honing pattern is destroyed and the cylinder must be rebored

8. Result of oil ring seizure. Engine must be rebored

9. Oil ring seizure here was not serious enough to warrant reboring. The honing marks are still visible

Cylinder wall damage
(© Daimler-Benz A.G.)

Visually inspect the cylinder bores for roughness, scoring, or scuffing. If evident, the cylinder bore must be bored or honed oversize to eliminate imperfections, and the smallest possible oversize piston used. The new pistons should be given to the machinist with the block, so that the cylinders can be bored or honed exactly to the piston size (plus clearance). If no flaws are evident, measure the bore diameter using a telescope gauge and micrometer, or dial gauge, parallel and perpendicular to the engine centerline, at the top (below the ridge) and bottom of the bore. Subtract the bottom measurements from the top to determine taper, and the parallel to the centerline measurements from the perpendicular measurements to determine eccentricity. If the measurements are not within specifications, the cylinder must be bored or honed, and an oversize piston installed. If the measurements are within specifications the cylinder may be used as is, with only finish honing (see below). NOTE: *Prior to submitting the block for boring, perform the following operation(s).*

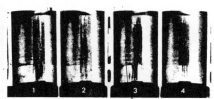

Cylinder bore measuring positions
(© Ford Motor Co.)

Measuring the cylinder bore with a telescope gauge
(© Buick Div. G.M. Corp.)

Determining the cylinder bore by measuring the telescope gauge with a micrometer
(© Buick Div. G.M. Corp.)

Measuring the cylinder bore with a dial gauge
(© Chevrolet Div. G.M. Corp.)

Procedure	Method
Check the block deck for warpage:	Using a straightedge and feeler gauges, check the block deck for warpage in the same manner that the cylinder head is checked (see Cylinder Head Reconditioning). If warpage exceeds specifications, have the deck resurfaced. NOTE: *In certain cases a specification for total material removal (Cylinder head and block deck) is provided. This specification must not be exceeded.*
* Check the deck height:	The deck height is the distance from the crankshaft centerline to the block deck. To measure, invert the engine, and install the crankshaft, retaining it with the center main cap. Measure the distance from the crankshaft journal to the block deck, parallel to the cylinder centerline. Measure the diameter of the end (front and rear) main journals, parallel to the centerline of the cylinders, divide the diameter in half, and subtract it from the previous measurement. The results of the front and rear measurements should be identical. If the difference exceeds .005″, the deck height should be corrected. NOTE: *Block deck height and warpage should be corrected concurrently.*
Check the cylinder block bearing alignment:  Checking main bearing saddle alignment (© Petersen Publishing Co.)	Remove the upper bearing inserts. Place a straightedge in the bearing saddles along the centerline of the crankshaft. If clearance exists between the straightedge and the center saddle, the block must be align-bored.
Clean and inspect the pistons and connecting rods:  Removing the piston rings (© Subaru)	Using a ring expander, remove the rings from the piston. Remove the retaining rings (if so equipped) and remove piston pin. NOTE: *If the piston pin must be pressed out, determine the proper method and use the proper tools; otherwise the piston will distort.* Clean the ring grooves using an appropriate tool, exercising care to avoid cutting too deeply. Thoroughly clean all carbon and varnish from the piston with solvent. CAUTION: *Do not use a wire brush or caustic solvent on pistons.* Inspect the pistons for scuffing, scoring, cracks, pitting, or excessive ring groove wear. If wear is evident, the piston must be replaced. Check the connecting rod length by measuring the rod from the inside of the large end to the inside of the small end using calipers (see

Procedure	Method

Cleaning the piston ring grooves
(© Ford Motor Co.)

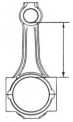

Connecting rod
length checking
dimension

illustration). All connecting rods should be equal length. Replace any rod that differs from the others in the engine.

* Have the connecting rod alignment checked in an alignment fixture by a machinist. Replace any twisted or bent rods.

* Magnaflux the connecting rods to locate stress cracks. If cracks are found, replace the connecting rod.

Fit the pistons to the cylinders:

Measuring the cylinder
with a telescope gauge
for piston fitting
(© Buick Div.
G.M. Corp.)

Measuring the piston
for fitting
(© Buick Div.
G.M. Corp.)

Using a telescope gauge and micrometer, or a dial gauge, measure the cylinder bore diameter perpendicular to the piston pin, $2\frac{1}{2}''$ below the deck. Measure the piston perpendicular to its pin on the skirt. The difference between the two measurements is the piston clearance. If the clearance is within specifications or slightly below (after boring or honing), finish honing is all that is required. If the clearance is excessive, try to obtain a slightly larger piston to bring clearance within specifications. Where this is not possible, obtain the first oversize piston, and hone (or if necessary, bore) the cylinder to size.

Assemble the pistons and connecting rods:

Installing piston pin lock rings
(© Nissan Motor Co., Ltd.)

Inspect piston pin, connecting rod small end bushing, and piston bore for galling, scoring, or excessive wear. If evident, replace defective part(s). Measure the I.D. of the piston boss and connecting rod small end, and the O.D. of the piston pin. If within specifications, assemble piston pin and rod. CAUTION: *If piston pin must be pressed in, determine the proper method and use the proper tools; otherwise the piston will distort.* Install the lock rings; ensure that they seat properly. If the parts are not within specifications, determine the service method for the type of engine. In some cases, piston and pin are serviced as an assembly when either is defective. Others specify reaming the piston and connecting rods for an oversize pin. If the connecting rod bushing is worn, it may in many cases be replaced. Reaming the piston and replacing the rod bushing are machine shop operations.

Procedure	*Method*

Clean and inspect the camshaft:

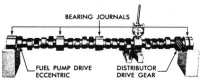

**Checking the camshaft
for straightness**
(© Chevrolet Motor
Div. G.M. Corp.)

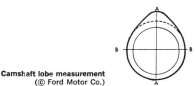

Camshaft lobe measurement
(© Ford Motor Co.)

Degrease the camshaft, using solvent, and clean out all oil holes. Visually inspect cam lobes and bearing journals for excessive wear. If a lobe is questionable, check all lobes as indicated below. If a journal or lobe is worn, the camshaft must be reground or replaced. NOTE: *If a journal is worn, there is a good chance that the bushings are worn.* If lobes and journals appear intact, place the front and rear journals in V-blocks, and rest a dial indicator on the center journal. Rotate the camshaft to check straightness. If deviation exceeds .001″, replace the camshaft.

* Check the camshaft lobes with a micrometer, by measuring the lobes from the nose to base and again at 90° (see illustration). The lift is determined by subtracting the second measurement from the first. If all exhaust lobes and all intake lobes are not identical, the camshaft must be reground or replaced.

Replace the camshaft bearings:

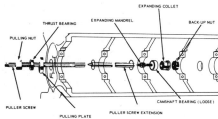

Camshaft removal and installation tool (typical)
(© Ford Motor Co.)

If excessive wear is indicated, or if the engine is being completely rebuilt, camshaft bearings should be replaced as follows: Drive the camshaft rear plug from the block. Assemble the removal puller with its shoulder on the bearing to be removed. Gradually tighten the puller nut until bearing is removed. Remove remaining bearings, leaving the front and rear for last. To remove front and rear bearings, reverse position of the tool, so as to pull the bearings in toward the center of the block. Leave the tool in this position, pilot the new front and rear bearings on the installer, and pull them into position. Return the tool to its original position and pull remaining bearings into position. NOTE: *Ensure that oil holes align when installing bearings.* Replace camshaft rear plug, and stake it into position to aid retention.

Finish hone the cylinders:

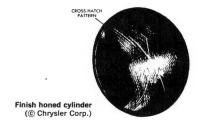

Finish honed cylinder
(© Chrysler Corp.)

Chuck a flexible drive hone into a power drill, and insert it into the cylinder. Start the hone, and move it up and down in the cylinder at a rate which will produce approximately a 60° cross-hatch pattern (see illustration). NOTE: *Do not extend the hone below the cylinder bore.* After developing the pattern, remove the hone and recheck piston fit. Wash the cylinders with a detergent and water solution to remove abrasive dust, dry, and wipe several times with a rag soaked in engine oil.

Procedure	Method
Check piston ring end-gap:  **Checking ring end-gap** (© Chevrolet Motor Div. G.M. Corp.)	Compress the piston rings to be used in a cylinder, one at a time, into that cylinder, and press them approximately 1″ below the deck with an inverted piston. Using feeler gauges, measure the ring end-gap, and compare to specifications. Pull the ring out of the cylinder and file the ends with a fine file to obtain proper clearance. CAUTION: *If inadequate ring end-gap is utilized, ring breakage will result.*
Install the piston rings:  PISTON RING FEELER GAGE RING GROOVE **Checking ring side clearance** (© Chrysler Corp.) 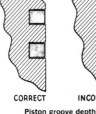 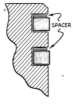 CORRECT INCORRECT SPACER **Piston groove depth** **Correct ring spacer installation**	Inspect the ring grooves in the piston for excessive wear or taper. If necessary, recut the groove(s) for use with an overwidth ring or a standard ring and spacer. If the groove is worn uniformly, overwidth rings, or standard rings and spacers may be installed without recutting. Roll the outside of the ring around the groove to check for burrs or deposits. If any are found, remove with a fine file. Hold the ring in the groove, and measure side clearance. If necessary, correct as indicated above. NOTE: *Always install any additional spacers above the piston ring.* The ring groove must be deep enough to allow the ring to seat below the lands (see illustration). In many cases, a "go-no-go" depth gauge will be provided with the piston rings. Shallow grooves may be corrected by recutting, while deep grooves require some type of filler or expander behind the piston. Consult the piston ring supplier concerning the suggested method. Install the rings on the piston, lowest ring first, using a ring expander. NOTE: *Position the ring markings as specified by the manufacturer (see car section).*
Install the camshaft:	Liberally lubricate the camshaft lobes and journals, and slide the camshaft into the block. CAUTION: *Exercise extreme care to avoid damaging the bearings when inserting the camshaft.* Install and tighten the camshaft thrust plate retaining bolts.
Check camshaft end-play:  **Checking camshaft end-play with a feeler gauge** (© Ford Motor Co.)	Using feeler gauges, determine whether the clearance between the camshaft boss (or gear) and backing plate is within specifications. Install shims behind the thrust plate, or reposition the camshaft gear and retest end-play.

Procedure	*Method*

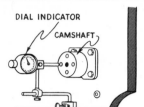

DIAL INDICATOR

CAMSHAFT

Checking camshaft end-play with a dial indicator

* Mount a dial indicator stand so that the stem of the dial indicator rests on the nose of the camshaft, parallel to the camshaft axis. Push the camshaft as far in as possible and zero the gauge. Move the camshaft outward to determine the amount of camshaft end-play. If the end-play is not within tolerance, install shims behind the thrust plate, or reposition the camshaft gear and retest.

Install the rear main seal (where applicable) :

Seating the rear main seal
(© Buick Div. G.M. Corp.)

Position the block with the bearing saddles facing upward. Lay the rear main seal in its groove and press it lightly into its seat. Place a piece of pipe the same diameter as the crankshaft journal into the saddle, and firmly seat the seal. Hold the pipe in position, and trim the ends of the seal flush if required.

Install the crankshaft :

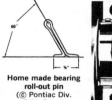

Home made bearing roll-out pin
(© Pontiac Div. G.M. Corp.)

INSTALLING BEARING SHELL

REMOVING BEARING SHELL

60-141

Removal and installation of upper bearing insert using a roll-out pin
(© Buick Div. G.M. Corp.)

Thoroughly clean the main bearing saddles and caps. Place the upper halves of the bearing inserts on the saddles and press into position. NOTE : *Ensure that the oil holes align.* Press the corresponding bearing inserts into the main bearing caps. Lubricate the upper main bearings, and lay the crankshaft in position. Place a strip of Plastigage on each of the crankshaft journals, install the main caps, and torque to specifications. Remove the main caps, and compare the Plastigage to the scale on the Plastigage envelope. If clearances are within tolerances, remove the Plastigage, turn the crankshaft 90°, wipe off all oil and retest. If all clearances are correct, remove all Plastigage, thoroughly

PRY FORWARD

THRUST BEARING

PRY CRANKSHAFT FORWARD

HOLD CRANKSHAFT FORWARD

PRY CAP BACKWARD

THRUST BEARING

PRY CAP BACKWARD

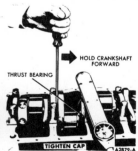

THRUST BEARING

HOLD CRANKSHAFT FORWARD

TIGHTEN CAP

A2879-A

Aligning the thrust bearing
(© Ford Motor Co.)

Procedure	*Method*
	lubricate the main caps and bearing journals, and install the main caps. If clearances are not within tolerance, the upper bearing inserts may be removed, without removing the crankshaft, using a bearing roll out pin (see illustration). Roll in a bearing that will provide proper clearance, and retest. Torque all main caps, excluding the thrust bearing cap, to specifications. Tighten the thrust bearing cap finger tight. To properly align the thrust bearing, pry the crankshaft the extent of its axial travel several times, the last movement held toward the front of the engine, and torque the thrust bearing cap to specifications. Determine the crankshaft end-play (see below), and bring within tolerance with thrust washers.
Measure crankshaft end-play:  **Checking crankshaft end-play with a dial indicator** (© Ford Motor Co.)  **Checking crankshaft end-play with a feeler gauge** (© Chevrolet Div. (G.M. Corp.))	Mount a dial indicator stand on the front of the block, with the dial indicator stem resting on the nose of the crankshaft, parallel to the crankshaft axis. Pry the crankshaft the extent of its travel rearward, and zero the indicator. Pry the crankshaft forward and record crankshaft end-play. NOTE: *Crankshaft end-play also may be measured at the thrust bearing, using feeler gauges* (see illustration).
Install the pistons:	Press the upper connecting rod bearing halves into the connecting rods, and the lower halves into the connecting rod caps. Position the piston ring gaps according to specifications (see car section), and lubricate the pistons. Install a ring compresser on a piston, and press two long (8″) pieces of plastic tubing over the rod bolts. Using the plastic tubes as a guide, press the pistons into the bores and onto the crankshaft with a wooden hammer handle. After seating the rod on the crankshaft journal, remove the tubes and install the cap finger tight. Install the remaining pistons in the same man-

Procedure	*Method*

**Tubing used as guide when installing
a piston**
(© Oldsmobile Div. G.M. Corp.)

ner. Invert the engine and check the bearing clearance at two points (90° apart) on each journal with Plastigage. NOTE: *Do not turn the crankshaft with Plastigage installed.* If clearance is within tolerances, remove *all* Plastigage, thoroughly lubricate the journals, and torque the rod caps to specifications. If clearance is not within specifications, install different thickness bearing inserts and recheck. CAUTION: *Never shim or file the connecting rods or caps.* Always install plastic tube sleeves over the rod bolts when the caps are not installed, to protect the crankshaft journals.

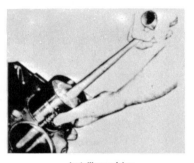

Installing a piston
(© Chevrolet Div. G.M. Corp.)

Check connecting rod side clearance:

Checking connecting rod side clearance
(© Chevrolet Div. G.M. Corp.)

Determine the clearance between the sides of the connecting rods and the crankshaft, using feeler gauges. If clearance is below the minimum tolerance, the rod may be machined to provide adequate clearance. If clearance is excessive, substitute an unworn rod, and recheck. If clearance is still outside specifications, the crankshaft must be welded and reground, or replaced.

Inspect the timing chain:

Visually inspect the timing chain for broken or loose links, and replace the chain if any are found. If the chain will flex sideways, it must be replaced. Install the timing chain as specified. NOTE: *If the original timing chain is to be reused, install it in its original position.*

Procedure	Method
Check timing gear backlash and runout:  **Checking camshaft gear backlash** (© Chevrolet Div. G.M. Corp.)  **Checking camshaft gear runout** (© Chevrolet Div. G.M. Corp.)	Mount a dial indicator with its stem resting on a tooth of the camshaft gear (as illustrated). Rotate the gear until all slack is removed, and zero the indicator. Rotate the gear in the opposite direction until slack is removed, and record gear backlash. Mount the indicator with its stem resting on the edge of the camshaft gear, parallel to the axis of the camshaft. Zero the indicator, and turn the camshaft gear one full turn, recording the runout. If either backlash or runout exceed specifications, replace the worn gear(s).

Completing the Rebuilding Process

Following the above procedures, complete the rebuilding process as follows:

Fill the oil pump with oil, to prevent cavitating (sucking air) on initial engine start up. Install the oil pump and the pickup tube on the engine. Coat the oil pan gasket as necessary, and install the gasket and the oil pan. Mount the flywheel and the crankshaft vibrational damper or pulley on the crankshaft. NOTE: *Always use new bolts when installing the flywheel.* Inspect the clutch shaft pilot bushing in the crankshaft. If the bushing is excessively worn, remove it with an expanding puller and a slide hammer, and tap a new bushing into place.

Position the engine, cylinder head side up. Lubricate the lifters, and install them into their bores. Install the cylinder head, and torque it as specified in the car section. Insert the pushrods (where applicable), and install the rocker shaft(s) (if so equipped) or position the rocker arms on the pushrods. If solid lifters are utilized, adjust the valves to the "cold" specifications.

Mount the intake and exhaust manifolds, the carburetor(s), the distributor and spark plugs. Adjust the point gap and the static ignition timing. Mount all accessories and install the engine in the car. Fill the radiator with coolant, and the crankcase with high quality engine oil.

Break-in Procedure

Start the engine, and allow it to run at low speed for a few minutes, while checking for leaks. Stop the engine, check the oil level, and fill as necessary. Restart the engine, and fill the cooling system to capacity. Check the point dwell angle and adjust the ignition timing and the valves. Run the engine at low to medium speed (800-2500 rpm) for approximately ½ hour, and retorque the cylinder head bolts. Road test the car, and check again for leaks.

Follow the manufacturer's recommended engine break-in procedure and maintenance schedule for new engines.

Chapter Four

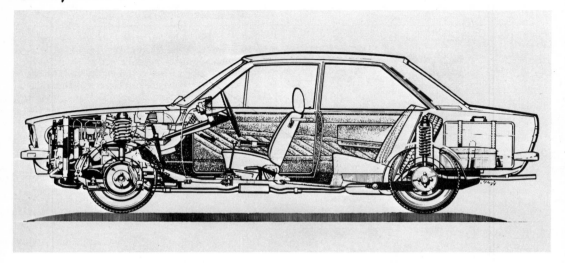

Emission Controls and Fuel System

Emission Controls

CRANKCASE VENTILATION

The purpose of the crankcase ventilation is twofold. It keeps harmful vapor byproducts of combustion from escaping into the atmosphere and prevents the building of crankcase pressure which can lead to oil leaks. Crankcase vapors are recirculated from the camshaft cover through a hose to the air cleaner. Here they are mixed with the air/fuel mixture and burned in the combustion chamber.

Service

The only maintenance required on the crankcase ventilation system is a periodic check. At every tune-up, examine the hoses for clogging or deterioration. Clean or replace the hoses as necessary.

EVAPORATIVE EMISSION CONTROL SYSTEM

This system prevents the escape of raw fuel vapors (unburned hydrocarbons or HC) into the atmosphere. Fuel when left in an unsealed tank, will evaporate, permitting its components to mix with the atmosphere. This causes an environmental hazard as the presence of these hydrocarbons is a threat to people who have to

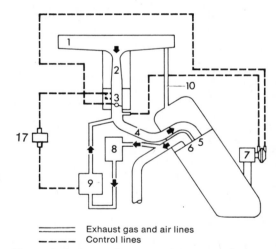

═══════	Exhaust gas and air lines
- - - - - -	Control lines

Fox emission control system schematic without air pump

1. Air cleaner	7. Distributor vacuum unit
2. Venturi	8. EGR filter
3. Throttle valve	9. EGR valve
4. Intake manifold	10. PCV line
5. Intake valve	17. Throttle delay valve
6. Exhaust valve	

breathe air with them mixed in it. In order to prevent this, the entire Fox's fuel system has been sealed so that the escaping vapors are drawn into a trap where they settle until they can be burned in the combustion process. The system consists of a sealed carburetor, unvented fuel tank filler cap, fuel tank expansion cham-

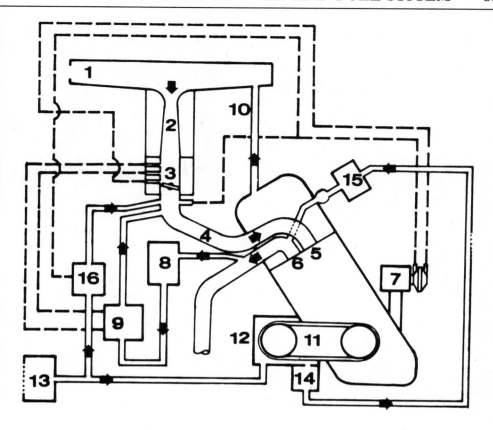

════════════ Exhaust gas and air lines

– – – – – – Control lines (vacuum)

Fox emission control system schematic with air pump

1. Air cleaner	9. Dual line EGR valve
2. Venturi	10. PCV line
3. Throttle valve	11. Air pump belt
4. Intake manifold	12. Air pump
5. Intake valve	13. Air pump filter
6. Exhaust valve	14. Pressure valve
7. Distributor vacuum unit	15. Check valve
8. EGR filter	16. Anti-backfire valve

Evaporative emissions control system charcoal filter

ber, an activated charcoal filter canister and connector hoses. Fuel vapors which reach the filter deposit hydrocarbons on the surface of the charcoal filter element. Fresh air enters the filter when the engine is running and forces the hydrocarbons to the air cleaner where they join the air/fuel mixture and are burned.

Service

Maintenance of the system consists of checking the condition of the various connector hoses and the charcoal filter at 10,000 mile intervals. The charcoal filter should be replaced at 50,000 mile intervals. It is located on the inside of the left fender at the bottom.

DUAL DIAPHRAGM DISTRIBUTOR

The purpose of the dual diaphragm distributor is to improve exhaust emissions during one of the engine's dirtier operating modes, idling. The distributor has a vacuum retard diaphragm, in addition to a vacuum advance diaphragm. The lower hose on the distributor vacuum unit is the retard hose; the upper hose is the advance hose.

Testing

1. Connect a timing light to the engine and check the ignition timing as described in Chapter 2, "Tune-Up and Troubleshooting."

2. Remove the retard hose from the distributor and plug it. Increase the engine speed. The ignition timing should advance. If it doesn't, then the vacuum unit is faulty and must be replaced.

EXHAUST GAS RECIRCULATION (EGR)

Exhaust gas recirculation is used primarily to lower the peak combustion temperatures and control the formation of nitrous oxide (NO_x). The amount of NO_x an engine emits at idle is not tremendously high, but when the engine is accelerating, or cruising at high speed, the combustion temperature goes over 2,500°F and the production of NO_x goes up proportionally.

To reduce NO_x emissions, metered amounts of cooled exhaust gases are added to the air/fuel mixture. The recirculated exhaust gas lowers the peak

EGR valve and vacuum line
9a. EGR valve   17. Throttle delay valve

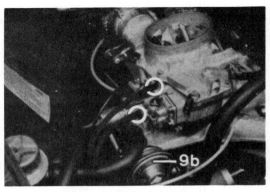

EGR valve and vacuum lines (California)
9b. EGR valve (Calif.)

flame temperature during combustion to cut the output of oxides of nitrogen. Exhaust gas from the manifold passes through a filter where it is cleaned. The vacuum-operated EGR valve controls the amount of this exhaust gas which is allowed into the intake manifold. There is no EGR at idle, partial at slight throttle, and full EGR at mid-to-full throttle. California Foxes are equipped with a dual chamber EGR valve.

Testing

ALL MODELS EXCEPT CALIFORNIA

1. Disconnect the vacuum line from the EGR valve.

2. Disconnect the vacuum hose from the distributor vacuum unit and extend hose.

3. Start the engine and allow it to idle.

4. Connect the distributor vacuum hose to the EGR valve. The engine should stumble or stall.

5. If the idle stays even, the EGR line is clogged or the EGR valve is defective.

CALIFORNIA

1. Disconnect both of the vacuum lines from the EGR valve.

2. Remove the retard hose (the lower one), from the distributor vacuum unit and place it on the other side of the engine.

3. Start the engine and let it idle.

4. Connect the distributor vacuum line to each of the EGR valves two connectors. The engine should not stumble or stall.

5. If the idle stays even during the

connection, the EGR line is clogged or the valve is defective. Clean the lines and repeat the test; if the same results are obtained, replace the EGR valve.

Maintenance

The only required maintenance is that the EGR filter be replaced at 20,000 mile (30,000 on 1975 models) or two year intervals.

1. Disconnect the filter EGR line fittings.
2. Remove the filter and discard.

EGR filter and lines

   6. EGR exhaust manifold connection
   8. EGR filter
   9. EGR valve

3. Install the new filter into the EGR lines and securely tighten fittings.

Removal and Installation

EGR VALVE

1. Disconnect the vacuum hose from the EGR valve.
2. Unbolt the EGR line fitting on the opposite side of the valve.
3. Remove the two retaining bolts and lift the EGR valve from the intake manifold.
4. Install the EGR valve in the reverse order of removal. Use a new gasket at the intake manifold.

AIR INJECTION

The air injection system, or air pump, is installed on 1974–75 California models. This system includes a belt-driven air pump, filter, check valve, anti-backfire valve or gulp valve, and connecting hoses and air lines. The pump, driven by a belt at the front of the engine, pumps air under a few pounds of pressure into each exhaust port. The hydrocarbons and car-

bon monoxide that comes out of the port are extremely hot and the contact with the injected air causes a flash in the exhaust manifold that combines the carbon monoxide with oxygen changing it into harmless carbon dioxide. There is a check valve in the system which keeps the hot exhaust gases from flowing back up the lines and into the pump, thus destroying it. The anti-backfire valve of the system shuts off the pump during deceleration to avoid damaging the exhaust system with a backfire. The valve basically redirects the forced air from the air pump away from the exhaust manifold during deceleration and into the intake manifold.

Maintenance

Required maintenance on the air pump consists of visually checking the pump, control valves, hoses and lines every 10,000 miles (15,000 miles on the 1975 models). Clean the air pump filter element at this interval. The filter element should be replaced every 20,000 miles or two years.

Testing and Service

1. Remove the air manifold from the engine and clean.

Air manifold retaining bolts

   S. Air manifold retaining bolts

2. Blow compressed air into the anti-backfire valve in the direction of the air-flow.

3. Clean or replace the air pump filter.

4. Start the engine.

5. Exhaust gas should flow equally from each air inlet.

6. With the engine idling, block the relief valve air outlet—only a slight pressure should be felt if the system is operating properly.

Anti-Backfire Valve

1. Disconnect the air pump filter line from the anti-backfire valve.

Anti-backfire valve (16) and connections

2. Briefly disconnect the anti-backfire valve vacuum line with the engine running. Air should be noticeably sucked in.

3. Replace the anti-backfire valve if the engine backfires.

HEATED AIR INTAKE SYSTEM

1973–74

All 1973–74 models have a heated air intake system, consisting of a tempera-

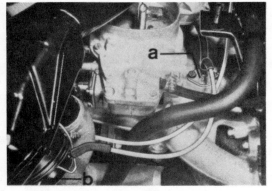

Intake manifold location of 1973 heated air intake temperature control valve

a. Temperature control valve   b. Vacuum unit

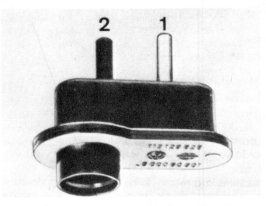

Example of a 1974 heated air intake temperature control valve, located in the air cleaner snout

1. Brass hose from the vacuum unit
2. Plastic hose from the carburetor

Air cleaner vacuum unit located on underside of air cleaner snout

1. Vacuum unit retaining clips (arrows)

ture control valve, a vacuum unit, and vacuum lines. The temperature control valve is located in the intake manifold on the 1973 and early 1974 models, and in the air cleaner in later 1974 models. The vacuum unit is located in the air cleaner snout and consists of a flap which allows either hot or cold air to enter the carburetor.

Control Valve Test

1. With the engine idling, pull the hose off the vacuum unit on the temperature control valve.

2. If the valve is operating properly, the flap which controls the warm airflow from the exhaust manifold must be closed.

3. If the flap in the air cleaner snout does not close, check the vacuum lines for leaks. If no leaks are found, remove

the vacuum unit from the air cleaner snout and clean it, then repeat the test. If the flap still doesn't close, replace the temperature control valve.

CATALYTIC CONVERTER

All 1975 California models are equipped with a catalytic converter located in the exhaust system. This device contains noble metals which act as catalysts, starting a reaction that converts hydrocarbons and carbon monoxide into water and carbon dioxide. The Fox is equipped with a catalytic converter light which will light at 30,000 mile intervals, at which time the converter must be replaced. All converter service should be performed by your authorized dealer. On a car with a catalytic converter, it is mandatory that unleaded gasoline be used. The use of leaded fuel will render the catalysts ineffective in dealing with the pollutants coming from the engine. Also be extremely careful not to touch the converter unit after the engine has been running, as it builds up high temperatures and can cause a severe burn if handled carelessly.

NOTE: *Do not try to determine if a plug is shorting out by removing the plug wire while the engine is running. Use an oscilloscope or you will damage the engine. Also, if you are having the car undercoated, be extremely careful not to get any undercoat on the catalytic converter because of the high temperatures the converter develops.*

Fuel System

MECHANICAL FUEL PUMP

The fuel pump works off an eccentric on the intermediate shaft. As the eccentric turns, it operates a diaphragm which sucks fuel from the tank and force feeds it to the carburetor. Inside the fuel pump is a filter screen which stops harmful substances from reaching the carburetor, at every tune-up this filter should be removed and cleaned.

NOTE: *All 1975 and later Foxes are equipped with electric fuel pumps mounted on the right-hand side of the fuel tank by the fender well.*

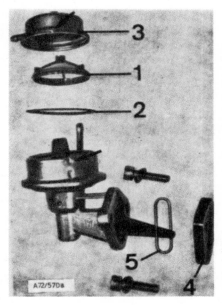

Exploded view of fuel pump

1. Screen	4. Plastic flange
2. Gasket	5. Flange seal
3. Cover	

Cleaning

The filter screen can be removed from the pump and cleaned.

1. Remove the center cover screw.
2. Remove the screen and gasket. Clean the screen in a safe solvent.
3. Replace the screen.
4. Install a new gasket and replace the cover.

NOTE: *Make sure that the depression in the pump cover engages the projection on the body of the pump.*

Removal and Installation

The Fox pump cannot be repaired and must be replaced when defective.

Fuel pump mounting

1. Disconnect and plug both fuel lines.
2. Remove the two socket head retaining bolts.
3. Remove the fuel pump and its plastic flange.
4. Replace the pump in the reverse order of removal. Use a new flange seal.

ELECTRIC FUEL PUMP

Removal and Installation

1. Remove and plug the necessary lines. Lines from other than the fuel tank should simply be drained into a suitable container.
2. Remove the pump electrical connector and remove the bracket mounting bolts along with the pump mounting bracket.
3. Loosen the clamping band screw and slide the pump out. The accumulator can also be removed now by disconnecting its connecting lines and loosening the clamping band around it, then sliding it out.

CARBURETOR

All 1974 models use a Solex 32/35 DIDTA carburetor with vacuum-controlled secondary throttle valve. The California model differs in some respects such as EGR vacuum pickup, and different idle system, but the carburetors are basically the same. The 1973 Fox uses a 32/35 TDID type Solex carburetor, which is basically similar to the 32/35 DIDTA version used on the 1974 models. The primary difference between the two is the size of the jets, the 1974 model having further modifications to reduce pollution.

Removal and Installation

1. Remove the air cleaner.
2. Disconnect the fuel line, being careful not to spill any fuel on the hot engine components.
3. Drain some of the coolant and then disconnect the choke hoses.
4. Disconnect the distributor and EGR valve vacuum lines.

Front view of a Solex 32/35 TDID carburetor

1. Choke housing cover	9. Idle jet	16. Cut-off valve
2. Retaining plate	10. Pump cover	17. Throttle lever
3. Choke housing	11. Pump lever	18. Vacuum advance connection line
4. Carburetor cover assembly	12. Carburetor body	23. Mounting screw
6. Cover screw	13. Mixture screw	24. Stop screw
7. Plug	14. Auxiliary fuel control screw	25. Choke connecting rod
8. Float chamber	15. Flange	26. Mounting screw

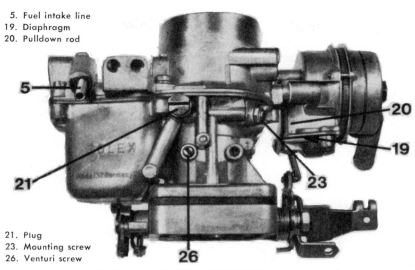

5. Fuel intake line
19. Diaphragm
20. Pulldown rod

21. Plug
23. Mounting screw
26. Venturi screw

Back view of a Solex 32/35 TDID carburetor

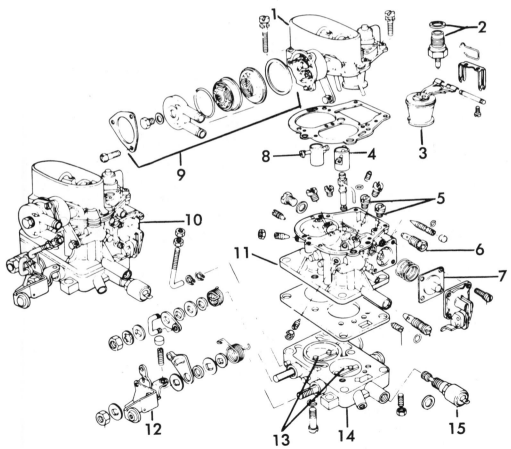

Exploded view of Solex 32/35 carburetor

1. Top housing	6. Idle jet	11. Carburetor bowl assembly
2. Float needle valve assembly	7. Accelerator pump assembly	12. Throttle lever assembly
3. Float	8. Venturi	13. Throttle valves
4. Venturi	9. Automatic choke assembly	14. Throttle plate
5. Main jets	10. Assembled view of carburetor	15. By-pass cutoff valve

5. Disconnect the electrical lead for the idle cut-off valve.

6. Remove the clip which secures the throttle linkage to the carburetor. Detach the linkage, being careful not to lose any washers or bushings.

7. Unbolt the carburetor from the manifold and remove it.

8. Use a new gasket when replacing the carburetor. Don't overtighten the nuts.

Aligning the external notches on an automatic choke

1. Choke cover notch
2. Adjuster ring notch
3. Choke housing notch

Automatic Choke Adjustment

The standard adjustment on all versions of the automatic choke is with the two notches aligned with the notch on the housing. To adjust, loosen the three clamping screws and move the outer part of the choke unit.

Internal Choke Adjustment

If after performing the above adjustment, the choke doesn't operate correctly, use the following procedure.

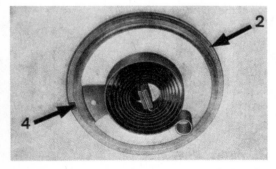

Internal components of the automatic choke: the control notch (2) is opposite the adjusting notch (4)

1. Remove the choke cover with coolant hoses attached and place out of the way.

2. The control notch (2) should be 180° opposite the adjusting notch (1). If not turn it with a screwdriver.

3. Reassemble the choke cover and adjust the choke as described above.

Dashpot Adjustment

1974 MODELS (EXCEPT CALIFORNIA)

1. Close the throttle valve, the choke must be fully open.

2. Press the plunger of the dashpot all the way in.

3. With the locknuts, adjust the dashpot gap tp $1/16$ in. (1 mm).

4. Open the throttle valve and fill the space between the locking ring and the bushing in the support bracket with shims.

Adjusting the dashpot gap "a" by turning adjusting screws "b"

Throttle Gap Adjustment

This adjustment is made with the carburetor removed.

1. Close the choke tightly. The stop lever should rest on the highest step of the stepped washer, holding the throttle open slightly.

2. Check the gap between lower edge of the throttle valve and the housing wall with a drill. The measurement should be:

Manual Transmission: 0.0255 in. (0.65 mm)

Auto. Transmission: 0.0314 in. (0.80 mm)

Checking the gap between the housing wall and the throttle valve with a bit

3. Adjust the primary gap by means of the two bolts on the connecting rod.

4. The secondary throttle should only be adjusted when it is definitely incorrectly adjusted. To adjust:

a. Loosen the adjusting screw until the throttle valve closes;

b. Turn the screw in ½ turn and lock;

c. Adjust idle mixture after this adjustment.

Choke Valve Gap Adjustment

1. Remove the choke cover and adjusting ring. Press the adjusting rod down to its stop.

Pressing the choke rod down

a. Choke rod

Checking the choke gap; note screwdriver still holding down choke rod

2. Check the choke gap for proper spacing, which is 0.137 ± 0.006 in. (3.5 ± 0.15 mm).

3. If adjustment is necessary, do so by bending the drive lever.

Throttle Linkage Adjustment

Throttle linkage adjustments are not normally required. However, it is a good idea to make sure that the throttle valve(s) in the carburetor open all the way when the accelerator pedal is held in the wide-open position. Only the primary throttle valve will open on the 32/35 DIDTA carburetor; the secondary throttle is vacuum-operated.

Overhaul

Efficient carburetion depends greatly on careful cleaning and inspection during overhaul since dirt, gum, water, or varnish in or on the carburetor parts are often responsible for poor performance.

Overhaul your carburetor in a clean, dust-free area. Carefully disassemble the carburetor, referring often to the exploded views. Keep all similar and look-alike parts segregated during disassembly and cleaning to avoid accidental interchange during assembly. Make a note of all jet sizes.

When the carburetor is disassembled, wash all parts (except diaphragms, electric choke units, pump plunger, and any other plastic, leather, fiber, or rubber parts) in clean carburetor solvent. Do not leave parts in the solvent any longer than is necessary to sufficiently loosen the deposits. Excessive cleaning may remove the special finish from the float bowl and choke valve bodies, leaving these parts unfit for service. Rinse all parts in clean solvent and blow them dry with compressed air or allow them to air dry. Wipe clean all cork, plastic, leather, and fiber parts with a clean, lint-free cloth.

Blow out all passages and jets with compressed air and be sure that there are no restrictions or blockages. Never use wire or similar tools to clean jets, fuel passages, or air bleeds. Clean all jets and valves separately to avoid accidental interchange.

Check all parts for wear or damage. If wear or damage is found, replace the defective parts. Especially check the following:

1. Check the float needle and seat for wear. If wear is found, replace the complete assembly.

2. Check the float hinge pin for wear and the float(s) for dents or distortion. Replace the float if fuel has leaked into it.

3. Check the throttle and choke shaft bores for wear or an out-of-round condition. Damage or wear to the throttle arm, shaft, or shaft bore will often require replacement of the throttle body. These parts require a close tolerance of fit; wear may allow air leakage, which could adversely affect starting and idling.

NOTE: *Throttle shafts and bushings are not included in overhaul kits. They can be purchased separately.*

4. Inspect the idle mixture adjusting needles for burrs or grooves. Any such condition requires replacement of the needle, since you will not be able to obtain a satisfactory idle.

5. Test the accelerator pump check valves. They should pass air one way but not the other. Test for proper seating by blowing and sucking on the valve. Replace the valve if necessary. If the valve is satisfactory, wash the valve again to remove breath moisture.

6. Check the bowl cover for warped surfaces with a straightedge.

7. Closely inspect the valves and seats for wear and damage, replacing as necessary.

8. After the carburetor is assembled, check the choke valve for freedom of operation.

Carburetor overhaul kits are recommended for each overhaul. These kits contain all gaskets and new parts to re-place those that deteriorate most rapidly. Failure to replace all parts supplied with the kit (especially gaskets) can result in poor performance later.

Some carburetor manufacturers supply overhaul kits of three basic types: minor repair; major repair; and gasket kits. Basically, they contain the following:

Minor Repair Kits:
  All gaskets
  Float needle valve
  Volume control screw
  All diaphragms
  Spring for the pump diaphragm
Major Repair Kits:
  All jets and gaskets
  All diaphragms
  Float needle valve
  Volume control screw
  Pump ball valve
  Float
  Complete intermediate rod
  Intermediate pump lever
  Some cover hold-down screws and
    washers
Gasket Kits:
  All gaskets

After cleaning and checking all components, reassemble the carburetor, using new parts and referring to the exploded view. When reassembling, make sure that all screws and jets are tight in their seats, but do not overtighten, as the tips will be distorted. Tighten all screws gradually, in rotation. Do not tighten needle valves into their seats; uneven jetting will result. Always use new gaskets. Be sure to adjust the float level when reassembling.

Some 1973–74 Foxes have had performance problems when making hard right-hand turns. This is caused by float malfunction in the carburetor. Audi has replaced the float with one that eliminates this problem and the parts for this modification, (a new float and needle valve gasket), are available from your local dealer.

If you own a 1974 Fox with an automatic transmission and have problems with a cold engine stalling when you place the transmission in Drive or Reverse, there is also a factory kit to eliminate this problem. The part number for this kit is 321-198-901. To install the kit:

1. Remove the air cleaner, carburetor and carburetor cover.

2. Replace the cover for the automatic choke vacuum piston. Connect the three pieces of hose and the Y fitting.

3. Install the carburetor cover.

4. Set the primary throttle gap to 1 mm (0.03 in.); set the choke valve gap to 3.6 mm (0.13 in.).

5. Replace the carburetor on the manifold.

6. Install the vacuum container about 1½ in. to the right of the hydraulic hood spring.

7. Install the vacuum solenoid and wiring harness under the front mounting bolt for the coil.

8. Before installing the vacuum solenoid, remove the insulator strip between the two terminals on the solenoid.

9. On cars where the ballast resistor is placed near the coil, a separate connecting wire with one male and one female lead has to be made. This should be made of 14 gauge wire and connected between the ballast unit hot side, and the vacuum solenoid harness. This procedure is not needed if the ballast resistor is located near the car's diagnostic plug.

10. Hook the thermo-switch to the T connector and install it with hoses into the hose going to the automatic choke housing.

11. Cut the vacuum advance line from the distributor at a suitable location and connect the thermo-switch using the hoses provided.

NOTE: *The angular vacuum pickup must face toward the automatic choke.*

12. Install the one-way valve from the kit; the center connection is to be connected to the vacuum solenoid with a long hose. Use the Y connector (supplied) if the T connector has no free vacuum lines.

13. Connect all vacuum lines, install the air cleaner and start the car in the manner outlined in the owner's manual.

AUDI CIS FUEL INJECTION

The 1975 Audi Fox is equipped with electronic fuel injection. Electronic fuel injection is a more precise way to monitor the needs of the engine and supply it with fuel accordingly. This system enables a car to meet stricter emissions control requirements without a large collection of economy-robbing additions to the carburetor. The Fox system, called CIS (Continuous Injection System), enables the Fox to meet the strict 1975 emissions regulations without the use of a catalytic converter except in California, where it is required.

Fox fuel injection unit

As the fuel is metered electronically to the cylinders, there is no adjustment possible on the unit, as part of the regular tune-up. There is, however, a key slot for adjustment on the "brain" of the unit but this shouldn't be touched except by an authorized mechanic with the proper equipment. Any tampering with the key slot will only increase the emissions level of the engine causing it to run poorly and pollute the air.

When doing a tune-up on a car equipped with CIS, it is very important that any vacuum lines which may have been disconnected during the tune-up process be reconnected. If there are any lines left open, the car will run poorly and cause you grief as you try to track down the source of the roughness.

Two types of CIS are used in 1975; they are basically similar except for the position of the "brain". The brain is the part of the system which receives the feedback from the engine and determines the amount of fuel to be sent to each cylinder. In early 1975 models, the brain is located on the right-side of the engine compartment near the firewall. This position necessitated moving the battery into the trunk. Later 1975 models have the "brain" located at the front of the engine compartment, and the battery on the right-side of the engine compartment near the firewall. The "brain" can be identified by the four wires going from the top of it to the intake manifold, and two to the fuel pump. If you are having any trouble with the fuel injection system, do not attempt to correct it yourself as you will only make matters worse; take the car to an authorized dealer who has the proper service tools.

Chapter Five

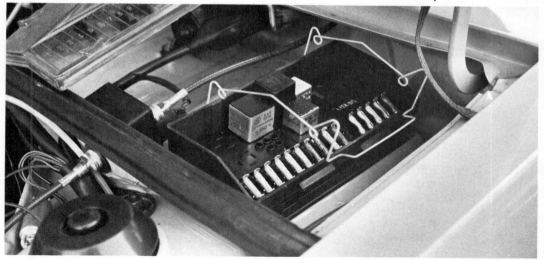

Chassis Electrical

Heater Unit

The heater core and blower are contained in the heater assembly which is removed and disassembled to service either component. The heater assembly is located in the passenger compartment under the center of the dash.

Removal and Installation

1. Disconnect the battery ground cable.
2. Drain the cooling system.
3. Remove the windshield washer container from its mounts. Remove the ignition coil.
4. Disconnect the two hoses from the heater core connections at the firewall.

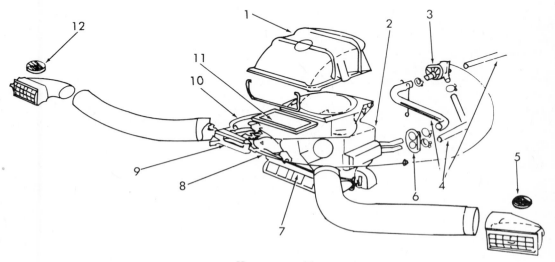

Heater assembly

1. Heater cover	5. Vent for side windows	9. Heater controls
2. Main heater assembly	6. Double grommet	10. Cutoff flap cable
3. Heater valve	7. Control flap cable	11. Fresh air housing
4. Heater hoses	8. Heater valve cable	12. Vent for side windows

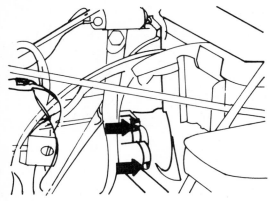

Heater core connections

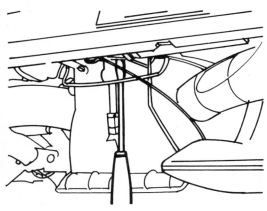

Removing heater controls

5. Unplug the electrical connector.

6. Remove the heater control knobs on the dash.

7. Remove the two retaining screws and remove the controls from the dash complete with brackets.

8. Pull the cable connection off the electric motor.

9. Disconnect the cable from the lever on the round knob.

10. Using a screwdriver, pry the retaining clip off the fresh air housing (the front portion of the heater.

11. Remove the fresh air housing complete with the controls.

12. Detach the left and right air hoses.

13. Remove the heater-to-dash panel mounting screws and lower the heater assembly.

14. Pull out the two pins and remove the heater cover. Unscrew and remove the fan motor.

15. Separate the heater halves to remove the heater core.

16. Installation is the reverse of removal. Refill the cooling system.

Radio

Removal and Installation

1. Remove the knobs from the radio.

2. Remove the nuts from the radio control shafts.

3. Detach the antenna lead from the jack on the radio case.

CAUTION: *Never operate the radio without a speaker; severe damage to the output transistors will result. If the speaker must be replaced, use a speaker of the correct impedance (ohms) or else the output transistors will be damaged and require replacement.*

4. Detach the power and speaker leads.

5. Remove the radio support nuts and bolts.

6. Withdraw the radio from beneath the dashboard.

7. Installation is performed in the reverse order of removal.

Windshield Wipers

BLADES

Replacement

When the windshield wiper blades have been exposed to the elements over a long period of time, it is good practice to replace them to ensure good vision in bad road conditions. Before purchasing the new set, measure the old ones to ensure a correct fit. Also be sure that the new set will fit the connection on the end of the wiper arm. The Fox's end connection is curved, so not all types of blades will fit it.

1. Pull the arms up off the windshield.

2. Press in on the plastic locking spring and slide the blade down off the wiper arm.

3. Hook on the new blade and pull up. This will engage the self locking spring.

4. Place the arms back flat on the windshield.

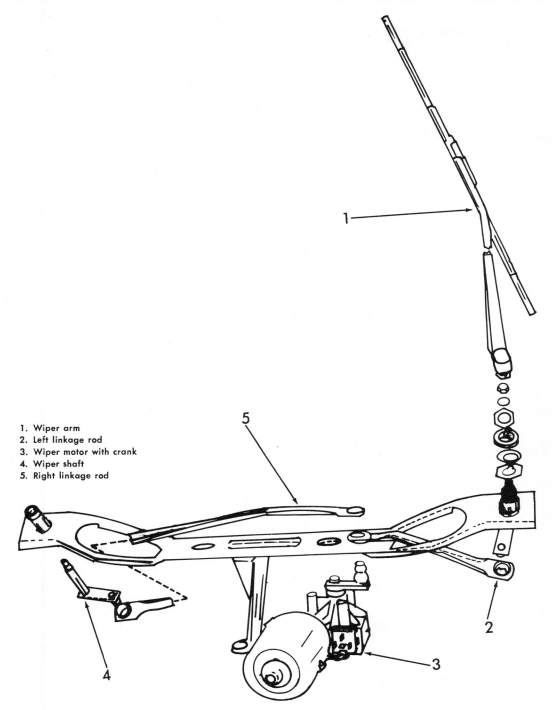

1. Wiper arm
2. Left linkage rod
3. Wiper motor with crank
4. Wiper shaft
5. Right linkage rod

Windshield wiper components

ARMS

Removal and Installation

1. Lift the blade and arm up off the windshield.

2. Simultaneously push the arm down and lift the smaller end cap up.

3. Remove the retaining nut and lift the arm off the shaft.

4. Install the arm in the reverse order

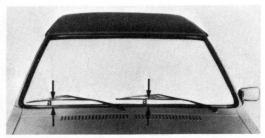

Wiper arm clearance should be distance "a": 1⅜ in. from the lower windshield molding

of removal. When properly installed, the blades should be 1⅜ in. from the lower windshield molding.

MOTOR

Removal and Installation

1. Remove the wiper arm; remove the retaining bolt on the cowl.

Windshield wiper linkage retaining bracket (arrow), and motor electrical connector plug (circle)

2. Unplug the electrical connector from the wiper motor.
3. Remove the three motor-to-linkage bracket retaining screws.

Windshield wiper crank arm at a right angle to the motor for proper installation

4. Carefully pry the motor crank out of the two linkage arms.
5. Drop the motor out of the car.
6. Install the motor in the reverse order of removal. The crank arm should be at a right angle to the motor as shown.

LINKAGE

The linkage is located under the hood directly in front of the firewall. It is removed from the engine side of the firewall.

Removal and Installation

The wiper linkage and motor can be dropped as a unit.
1. Remove the wiper arms as described above.
2. Unplug the electrical connector from the wiper motor.
3. Remove the large hex nuts from the linkage shafts.
4. Remove the covers and slotted washers.
5. After removing the linkage bracket retaining bolt, drop the entire linkage assembly down and out of the car.
6. The individual links are removed by prying them off the shaft links with a screwdriver.
7. Install the wiper linkage in the reverse order of removal. Lubricate the shafts with the multipurpose chassis grease before installation.

Instrument Cluster

Removal and Installation

1. Disconnect the battery negative cable and remove the lower dash panel.

Retaining springs and electrical connections behind the instrument panel

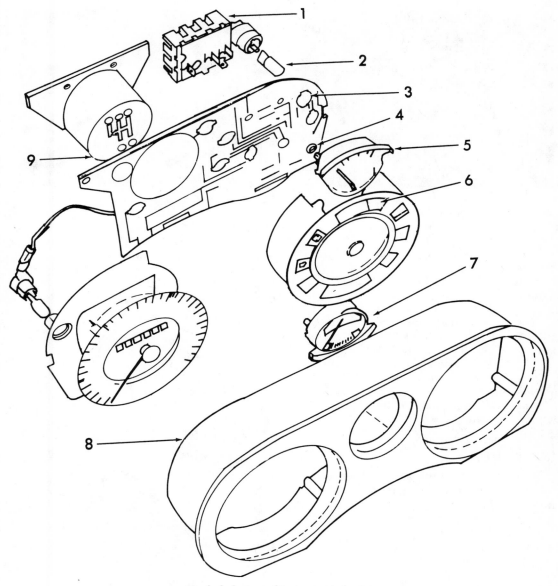

Exploded view of instrument cluster

1. Voltage stabilizer
2. Bulb
3. Printed circuit board
4. Washer
5. Fuel gauge
6. Trim plate
7. Coolant temperature gauge
8. Instrument cluster
9. Cover

2. Unscrew the speedometer cable from the rear of the cluster.

3. Using needlenose pliers, detach the retaining springs on either side of the cluster. (See arrows on illustration.)

4. Pivot the instrument cluster out of the dash.

5. Disconnect the electrical connector plug at the rear of the cluster.

6. Remove the cluster from the dash.

7. Installation is the reverse of removal.

SPEEDOMETER CABLE

1. Unscrew the speedometer cable from the rear of the instrument cluster.

2. Unsnap the rubber grommets from the dash panel support and the firewall.

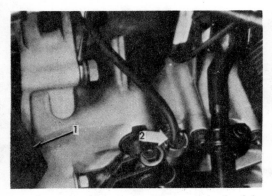

Speedometer cable attaching point, in back of the oil filter, on the transaxle

1. Oil filter   2. Speedometer cable

3. Pull the speedometer cable through the holes.

4. Use pliers to unscrew the cable from the transaxle.

5. Installation is the reverse of removal. The correct lengths for the replacement cables are 49.2 in. for manual cars and 55.1 in. for automatic cars.

NOTE: *When installing the speedometer cable, make sure that there are no kinks in it and that it has not been squeezed thus preventing the cable from turning.*

TROUBLESHOOTING THE INSTRUMENTS

If your instruments are reading erratically, it may be because of two brass nuts at the back of the instrument cluster working loose and shorting out the instruments. To correct this condition, remove the instrument cluster as previously outlined and tighten the nuts. Also while back there, check any other connections for possible looseness or wires which may be touching each other and shorting out.

Headlights

Removal and Installation

1. Loosen the grille retaining screws and remove the grille.

2. Remove the chrome trim ring mounting screws and tilt the light and ring forward.

Headlight attaching screws (arrows)

3. Pull off the connector plug.

4. Attach a new headlight to the connector plug; make sure that the lettering on the trim ring is at the top of the headlight and that the lettering on the face of the bulb is at the bottom of the bulb.

Lettering on the bulb at the bottom; lettering on the trim ring at the top for proper headlight installation

5. Attach the trim ring retaining screws and reattach the grille.

FUSES

The fuses and relays are located in the engine compartment, on the left-side near the firewall, under the plastic fuse cover. Each fuse's function is marked on the plastic cover. They are of three different amperages: 8, 16, and 25 amps.

Fox fuse box with fuse positions marked on the plastic cover

Fuse Identification

8 amp fuses—White
16 amp fuses—Red
25 amp fuses—Blue

Fuse Chart

Fuse Number	Function	Amperage
1.	Low beam left	8
2.	Low beam right	8
3.	High beam left	8
4.	High beam right and high beam indicator light	8
5.	Back-up light and heater fan	8
6.	Horn	8
7.	Turn signals and emergency flasher lights	8
8.	Rear window defogger	16
9.	Windshield wiper motor and cigarette lighter	16
10.	Stop lights, interior light (shift pattern) or clock	8
11.	Windshield wiper switch	16
12.	Windshield washer switch	16
13.	Taillight, right parking light license plate light	8
14.	Taillight, left parking light	8
15.	Instrument lights	8
16.	Air conditioner	25
17.	Empty	—

Relay Chart

1973-74

A. Electric radiator fan
B. Headlights
C. Dimmer relay for high beams
D. Turn signals
E. Windshield wipers
F. Rear window defogger
G. Air conditioner (optional)

1975

A. None (bridged for radiator fan)
B. Vacant
C. Dimmer relay for high beams
D. Turn signal-emergency flasher
E. Turn signal
F. None (bridged for windshield wiper system)
G. Vacant
H. Vacant
I. Rear window defogger
J. Vacant

NOTE: *Relay code letter is stamped on the fuse box cover.*

Light Bulb Specifications

Function	Replacement Bulb
Sealed beam headlights	6014
Front turn signals and parking lights	1034
Side marker lights	57
Rear turn signals	57
Stop lights	1073
Taillights	1073
Back-up lights	1073
License plate lights	N17 726 2 °
Light switches	N17 751 2 °
Dash instrument, indicator, and warning lights	194
Instrument illuminator, indicator, and warning lights	194
Glove compartment light	N17 722 2 °
Interior light	N17 723 2 °

° Audi part numbers

Wiring Diagrams

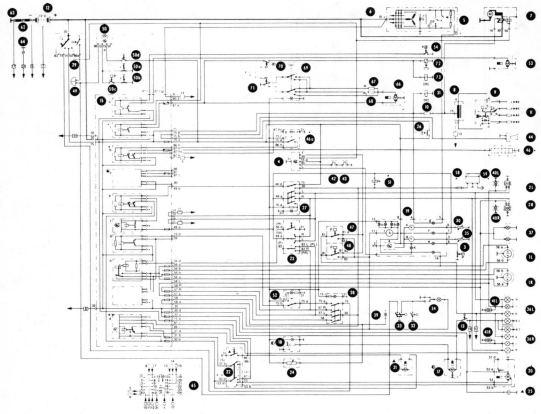

1973 Fox with manual transmission

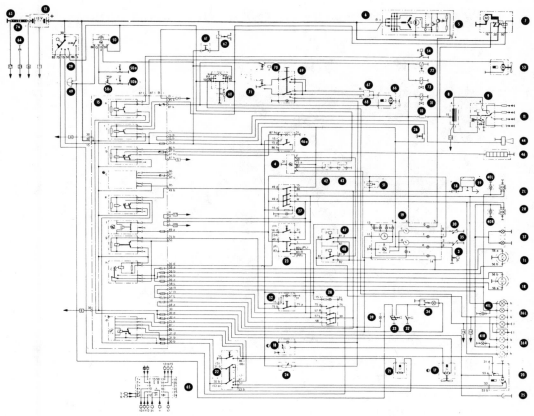

1973 Fox with automatic transmission

Chapter Six

Clutch and Transaxle

Manual Transaxle

Shift Lever Adjustment

1973–74

1. Shift the transmission into Neutral and remove the gearshift boot and the oval shift lever cover.

2. Loosen the two screws on top and move the lever into the right-hand side of the lever area (Third and Fourth gear area).

3. Tighten the screws and move the lever to the left (First and Second gear area), and back to the right. If the lever is tight or jams, lubricate the lever plate to free it.

4. Next, from underneath the car, loosen the two shift plate bolts and adjust the plate backward and forward to obtain maximum smoothness.

5. When the gearshift lever moves freely, tighten the bolts.

1975

A new gearshift mechanism has been installed in all Foxes starting with chassis serial number 8 52007172. The procedure for adjusting it is different from the preceding years:

1. Place the gearshift lever in Neutral.

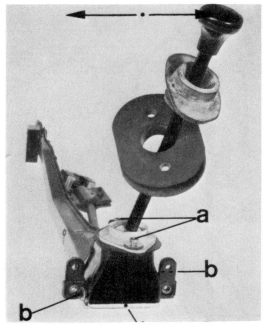

Manual transaxle shift lever adjustment

a. Side movement screws
b. Shift plate bolts for forward and back adjustment

2. From underneath the car, remove the shift rod coupling clamp.

3. Check that the shift finger slides freely on the shift rod.

4. Remove the console.

5. Align the centering holes (front

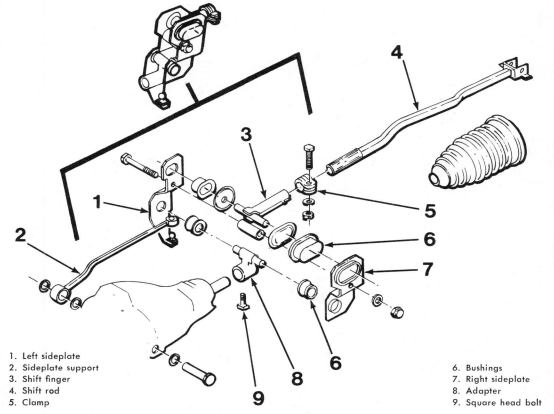

1. Left sideplate
2. Sideplate support
3. Shift finger
4. Shift rod
5. Clamp

6. Bushings
7. Right sideplate
8. Adapter
9. Square head bolt

1975 gearshift mechanism

and rear of the shift lever) of the gearshift lever bearing and the gearshift lever housing; tighten the bolts.

6. Install a jig with its locating pin toward the front.

7. Eliminate any play in the shift lever ball halves by lifting up the gearshift lever and pushing down on the jig at the same time.

8. Secure the jig position by tightening the curled screw.

9. Check that the shift finger slides freely and then install the clamp bolt and nut and tighten.

10. Check that all the gears engage without jamming; if necessary, move the shift lever bearing sideways.

Axle Shaft (Halfshaft) Removal and Installation

1. With the car on the ground, remove the axle shaft nut. This nut is torqued on very tightly, so a bar on the end of the wrench may be necessary to break it loose.

The axle shaft nut, torqued to 137 ft lbs

2. With the front of the car raised, remove the socket head bolts. If the right-side driveshaft is to be removed, the exhaust pipe must be removed from the exhaust manifold and from the support bracket on the transmission.

3. Pull the driveshaft out and lay it up on the transaxle.

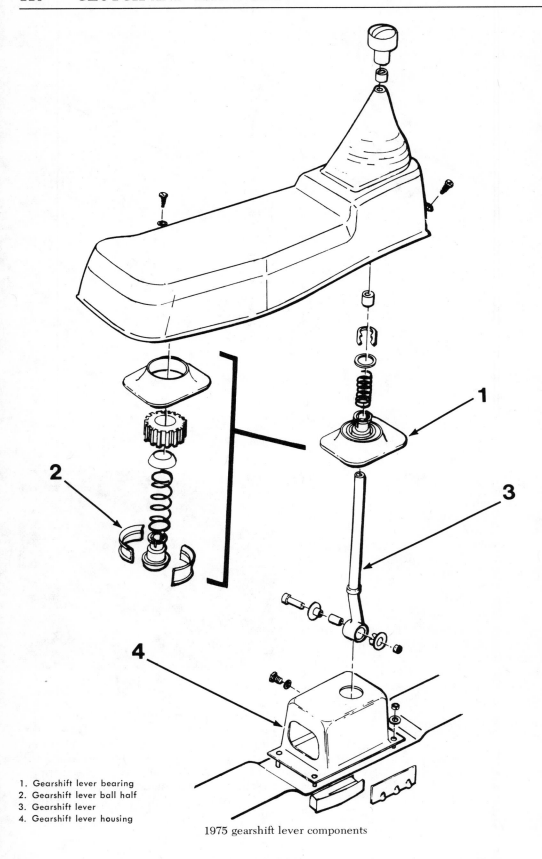

1. Gearshift lever bearing
2. Gearshift lever ball half
3. Gearshift lever
4. Gearshift lever housing

1975 gearshift lever components

Removing the driveshaft socket head bolts

Removing the driveshaft from the steering knuckle

Exhaust pipe support bracket on right-side of car

1. Gearshift rod bolt
2. Exhaust pipe-to-transaxle bolt
3. Transaxle mounting bolt
4. Transaxle mounting bolt

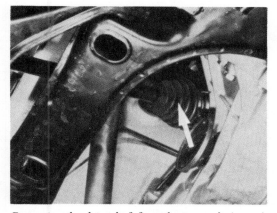

Removing the driveshaft from the transaxle (arrow)

4. With the steering locked, pull the other end of the driveshaft out of the steering knuckle.

5. On Foxes with automatic transmissions, when removing the left-side axle shaft mark the position of the ball joint on the track control arm to avoid having to readjust the camber angle later in the operation.

6. Press the pivot mounting outward and remove the driveshaft being careful not to damage the brake hoses.

7. Installation is the reverse of removal. Tighten the transaxle bolts to 25 ft lbs; the axle nut is tightened to 137 ft lbs.

Removal and Installation

1. Disconnect the battery ground cable and raise the car on a ramp or lift.

2. Disconnect the exhaust system and move it to the right, out of the way. It would be a good idea to hang it from a bracket with wire to keep it from dangling.

3. Remove the driveshafts. See "Axle Shafts."

4. Disconnect the speedometer cable and remove the starter.

5. Remove the transmission-to-engine bolts as shown in Chapter 3.

6. Disconnect the gearshift rod and remove the transmission mounting bolts.

7. Disconnect the back-up light switch wires and remove the bolts from the gearshift bracket.

8. Ease the transmission back away from the engine and lower it out of the car.

9. Installation is the reverse of removal but remember to reconnect the back-up light wires before installing the rear transmission mounting bracket; also before installing the rear mounting bracket, tighten the set screw for the gearshift rod and hold it in place with wire to aid in installation.

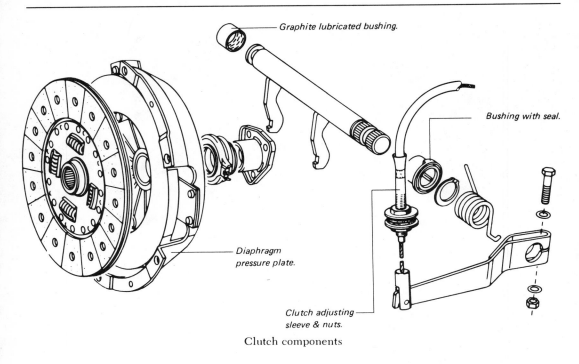

Clutch components

Clutch

A clutch is a system of parts making up a friction device which is used to connect and disconnect a driving force (the engine) from a driven member (the driveshaft). An engine develops little torque or driving force at low rpm and must therefore gain sufficient speed before it will drive the car. If this rapidly rotating engine were to be connected directly to the drive train, it would tear the drive train up, so some way must be provided for the engine and drive train to engage in order to move the car without destroying the drive train. In cars with manual transmissions, this is accomplished by the use of a clutch. The clutch enables the engine to gradually connect with the transmission in order to provide a smooth start. When the clutch pedal is pushed in (disengaged), the rotating motion of the engine is separated from the transmission, which makes it much easier to shift gears in the transmission. When disengaged, a cable attached to the clutch pedal pulls on the clutch release lever. This causes the clutch release (throwout) bearing (connected to the release lever),

to press against the release levers of the pressure plate. This action removes the spring pressure of the pressure plate from the clutch disc. Since it was this pressure that was holding the clutch disc against the engine flywheel, the clutch can now move away from the flywheel. If the engine torque is to be transmitted to the rest of the drive train, the clutch must be held firmly against the flywheel. By depressing the clutch pedal, you allow the clutch disc to move away from the flywheel, separating the engine power from the drive train.

Pedal Free-Play Adjustment

Free-play in the clutch pedal is the amount of distance the pedal will travel before the linkage starts to move the throwout bearing. It is necessary to adjust it because of the normal stretching of the clutch cable and the wearing of the clutch disc. The proper pedal free-play should be about ⅝ in. (15 mm).

1. With your hand, move the clutch pedal and check for the proper free-play.

2. If the free-play is more or less than ⅝ in., it must be adjusted. To increase the free-play, loosen the lower nut and tighten the top one; to decrease the free-

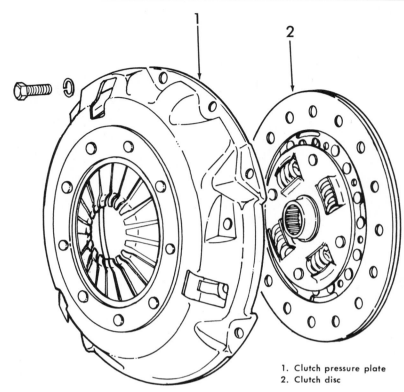

1. Clutch pressure plate
2. Clutch disc

Exploded view of clutch assembly

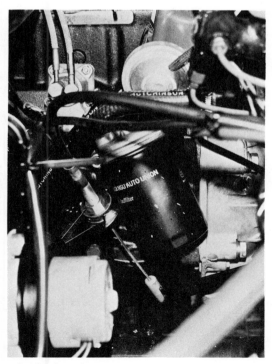

Clutch adjusting nuts

play, loosen the top nut and tighten the bottom one.

3. After the free-play has been adjusted, tighten whichever nut has been loosened.

Clutch Cable Replacement

1. Loosen both of the clutch adjusting nuts.

2. Remove the clutch cable from the clutch pedal.

3. Slide the clutch cable out of the clutch bracket and remove the clutch cable from the operating lever.

4. Installation is the reverse of removal, but remember when finished to adjust the free-play.

Clutch Release Lever Replacement

1. Remove the clutch release bearing (throwout bearing), by unsnapping the retaining clips and sliding it off the bearing shaft.

2. Loosen the clamp bolt and remove the operating lever.

3. Remove the snap-ring (left-side),

and retaining bolt (right-side), from the release lever.

4. Remove the bushing by sliding the operating shaft to the left.

5. Remove the operating shaft by sliding it to the right.

6. Clean and check all parts for wear, lubricate the shaft and install in the reverse order of removal, but note the position of the operating lever as shown. *It must be aligned this way.*

Proper alignment of the clutch operating lever

Removal and Installation

1. Remove the transaxle as described in Chapter 3.

2. Make a mark on the flywheel and the pressure plate to aid in alignment later on if the pressure plate is to be reused.

3. Unscrew the pressure plate bolts one at a time, working diagonally opposite each other rather than simply unscrewing them haphazardly. This criss-cross pattern ensures that the spring pressure will not warp the pressure plate.

4. When the spring pressure is completely released, remove the bolts entirely and separate the pressure plate and disc.

5. Once taken apart, the pressure plate and flywheel should be cleaned in a suitable (non-oil based) solvent. Check the spring ends (where the release bearing contacts) for wear. The permissible level for wear on them is 0.01 in. (0.3 mm). The friction surface of the flywheel (where the clutch disc contacts) should be checked for cracks, burn marks or wear; a taper on the inside edge of 0.01 in. (0.3 mm) is alright. Check the pressure plate rivets for tightness, if any are loose, replace the pressure plate. The clutch disc and release bearing should

Check the spring ends of the clutch for wear

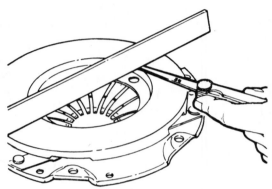

Check the pressure plate surface for distortion which shouldn't be more than 0.012 in. (0.3 mm)

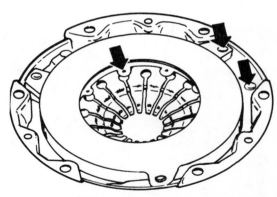

Check the pressure plate for surface wear. Make sure that the cover straps are not cracked or the rivets loose

always be replaced when the clutch is taken apart.

6. Make sure that all the parts which are to be assembled are clean. Don't clean the disc in solvent, just wipe it off with a clean, lint-free cloth.

7. Insert the clutch disc and pressure plate, making sure that the mark on the plate lines up with the flywheel mark.

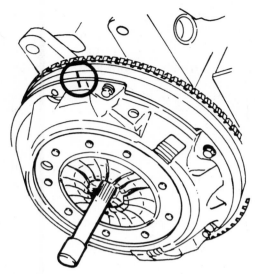

Aligning clutch disc—note aligned matchmarks

8. Center the disc with a pilot shaft or an old transaxle shaft which can be picked up at a local junkyard.

9. Gradually tighten the pressure plate-to-flywheel bolts in a criss-cross pattern, torquing them to 18 ft lbs.

10. Install the release bearing by sliding it into place and replacing the retaining clips.

11. Reinstall the transaxle on the engine as described in Chapter 3.

Automatic Transaxle

All of the normal maintenance such as checking the fluid levels and changing the filter are covered in Chapter 1. The halfshaft (driveshaft) removal and installation procedures are the same as those for the manual transaxle. This section will include checks that can be made with the transaxle assembled. Overhauling an automatic transaxle requires special tools and skills not normally possessed by the "at-home" mechanic, so this should be left to a qualified shop.

Since the automatic transaxle can be lowered from the car with the engine left in place, it will be included here as it is possible to obtain a rebuilt transaxle and install it yourself.

Removal and Installation

1. Disconnect the battery ground cable.

2. Raise the car on a chassis hoist.

3. Remove the lockplates and remove the axle shaft bolts. Wire the shafts up out of the way.

4. Disconnect the vacuum hose and remove the torque converter guard plate; disconnect the kick-down switch wire.

5. Unscrew the speedometer cable nut from the transaxle case using a pair of pliers.

6. Support the transaxle with a transmission jack and remove the upper torque converter bolts through the starter opening. It may be necessary to use a large screwdriver as a wedge to prevent the flywheel from moving when doing this.

7. Unbolt the small crossmember at the rear of the transaxle; remove the exhaust pipe bracket.

8. Lower the transaxle slightly and remove the shift linkage at the transaxle.

NOTE: *When replacing the shift cable, always replace the circlip and O-ring from where the cable joins the transaxle.*

9. Remove the lower engine-to-transaxle bolts.

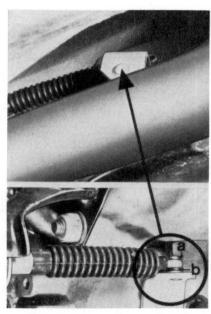

Shift linkage cable on the transaxle (bottom circle is close up)

a. Circlip   b. O-ring

10. Separate the transaxle from the engine and lower it. The torque converter should be held in place in the transaxle by a strap.

11. Installation is the reverse of removal, torque the engine-to-transaxle bolts to 40 ft lbs and the torque converter bolts to 20–23 ft lbs. New torque converter bolts must always be used. The axle shaft bolts must be torqued to 28 ft lbs.

12. Check the shift linkage adjustment.

Cable and Linkage Adjustment

The shift lever linkage must be adjusted properly in order for the transaxle to perform smoothly. The engine should be warmed up before attempting to adjust the linkage.

1. Place the gearshift lever in Neutral, the parking brake on, and let the engine run at 1,000–1,200 rpm.

2. Move the lever to the Reverse position. The engine speed must drop when this happens.

3. Move the lever into Park, the engine speed should rise as the transaxle is disengaged.

4. Repeat Step 2, the results should be the same.

5. Move the lever to Neutral, the engine speed should rise when the transaxle is disengaged.

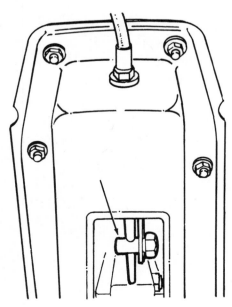

Automatic transmission linkage adjustment

6. Move the lever to the Drive position. When the transaxle is engaged the engine speed should drop.

7. Move the lever all the way back to First gear. It should go into First with no resistance.

8. If there is an adjustment necessary, place the lever in Park and remove the cover from the bottom of the shift lever case under the car.

9. Loosen the cable clamp and have an assistant hold the transaxle lever all the way against the rear stop. When in place, tighten the clamp.

10. Repeat Steps 1–7 after replacing the cover on the case.

Checking the Kick-Down Switch

1. Turn the ignition switch on, but don't start the engine.

2. Floor the accelerator pedal; there should be a click from the kick-down switch solenoid on the transaxle if it's working properly.

3. If there is no sound, have the solenoid replaced.

Neutral Safety Switch

The neutral safety switch prevents the engine from being started with the transaxle in any position other than Park or Neutral. The switch is at the base of the shift lever, inside the console.

1. Remove the four console retaining screws.

2. Place the gearshift lever in Neutral and remove the two screws which hold the shift position indicator plate to the console. Remove the shift knob and console.

3. Disconnect the switch electrical leads.

4. Remove the two switch retaining screws. The back-up light wires are at the front.

5. Install the new switch so that the contacts are together.

6. Install the electrical connectors. Put the handbrake on and attempt to start the engine in Neutral and Park. It should start in these positions only. Make sure that the back-up lights operate only in Reverse. If the switch does not operate properly, loosen the screws and move it in its slotted mounting bracket until it is operating properly.

7. Replace the console cover.

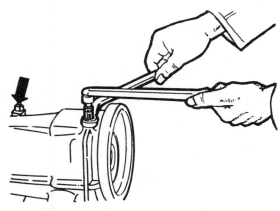

Adjusting front (First gear) band—arrow locates Second gear band adjustment screw

First Gear (Front) Band Adjustment

NOTE: *The transmission must be horizontal when both this and the following adjustment are performed. The first gear band has a narrow point adjusting screw, the second gear band a wide screw.*

1. Tighten the first gear band adjusting screw to 7 ft lbs (84 in. lbs).

2. Loosen the screw and tighten it again to 3.5 ft lbs (42 in. lbs).

3. Turn the screw out 3¼–3½ turns and then tighten the locknut.

Second Gear (Rear) Band Adjustment

1. Tighten the second gear band adjusting screw to 7 ft lbs (84 in. lbs).

2. Loosen the screw and tighten it again to 3.5 ft lbs (42 in. lbs).

3. Turn the screw out 2½ turns and then tighten the locknut.

Transaxle Codes

1973	Manual	ZV
	Automatic	ZW
1974	Manual	ZS
	Automatic	ZW
1975	Manual	YZ
	Automatic	EO

Chapter Seven

Suspension and Steering

Front Suspension

The Audi Fox front suspension is a MacPherson strut type. The shock absorber, which is located inside the coil spring, is used to locate or position the suspension assembly. The use of this type suspension means that no upper control arm is necessary, as the shock-coil spring unit handles this function. The other parts of this suspension include a lower control arm and ball joint, along with a stabilizer bar to keep the front end steady in turns.

BALL JOINTS

Ball joints are spherical connecting links of a ball and socket type in which a ball, on the end of a stud, rides inside a socket assembly, which is in turn, attached to the lower control arm. The ball joints function is to act as a pivot point to enable the front wheels to turn in response to the steering wheel, and to compensate for changes in the road surface such as bumps, and their accompanying rebounds, which would affect the steering. The Fox does not use an upper ball joint assembly, that function being taken care of by the strut.

Removal and Installation

1. Jack up the front of the car and support it properly under the center of the subframe or at the side, on the jacking plate.
2. Make a mark on the ball joint flange and a matching one on the control arm for later alignment.
3. Remove the upper retaining nut and bolt.
4. Pry the lower control arm and ball joint down and out of the strut.
5. Remove the two ball joint flange-to-lower control arm retaining nuts and bolts.

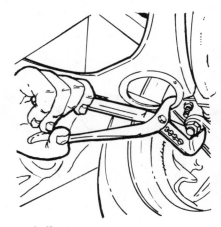

Aligning ball joint

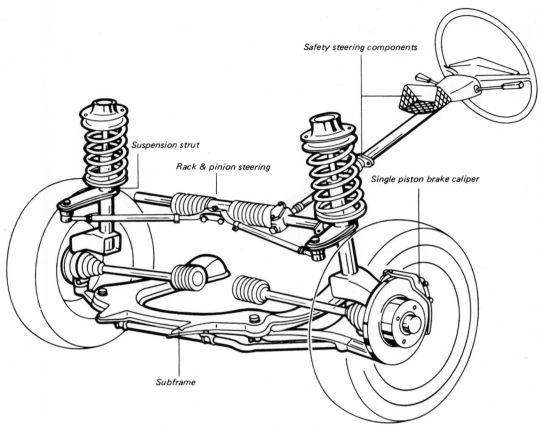

Safety steering components

Suspension strut

Rack & pinion steering

Single piston brake caliper

Subframe

Front suspension and steering components

6. Remove the ball joint assembly.

7. The ball joint is installed in the reverse order of removal, and if no new parts were installed, simply align the marks made in Step 2 to install, as no camber alignment is necessary.

8. Pull the ball joint into alignment with a pair of pliers. Tighten the two control arm bolts to 47 ft lbs and the strut-to-ball joint bolt to 18 ft lbs.

If new parts have been used, refer to "Camber Adjustment" in this chapter.

SHOCK ABSORBERS

The function of a shock absorber is to dampen the harsh movement of the car's springs and to provide a means of dispersing the movements of the wheels so that the shocks encountered by the wheels are not completely transmitted to the body of the car. As each wheel moves up and down, the shock absorber expands and contracts, imposing a restraint on car body movement by its hydraulic action.

The operating principle of hydraulic shock absorbers is one of forcing fluid through restricting openings in a series of valves. The restricted flow slows down the rapid motion of the car's springs as they encounter irregularities in the road surface. The shock adjusts itself to the severity of the motion it receives; a light up and down motion would cause the fluid to meet little resistance, while a harder bounce or series of bumps would cause the resistance to be higher creating a more stable ride over obstacles. A double-acting shock absorber simply means that a shock acts in both directions, dampening the spring on the rebound as well as the upstroke.

A simple way to see if your shock absorbers are functioning correctly is to push one corner of the car down a few times. This will compress the spring on that side of the car as well as the shock absorber. If the shock absorber is functioning properly, it will control the spring's tendency to remain in motion.

Thus the car will level itself almost instantly when you release the downward pressure. If the car continues to bounce up and down several times, the shock absorber is worn out and should be replaced. Examine the strut body for heavy oil streaking, which would indicate shock leakage. Replace a leaky shock absorber.

Removal and Installation

Since the shock absorber cartridge is contained within the strut assembly, it's necessary to remove the strut and then the coil spring in order to remove the shock. We recommend removing the strut yourself and then taking the assembly to a dealer or spring shop to have the spring compressed and removed and the new shock absorber cartridge installed. On this job, since the removal and installation of the strut is the major labor charge, you'll save part of the expense and avoid the danger of an accident when compressing the spring.

STRUT

Removal and Installation

1. With the car resting on the ground, remove the front axle nut. Loosen the wheel lug bolts.

2. Raise and support the front of the car securely, then remove the wheels.

3. Remove the brake caliper and position it out of the way so that it won't be damaged. The factory recommends that you hang it with wire from the control arm.

4. Remove the brake line clip from the strut.

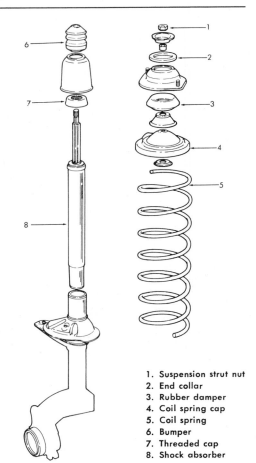

1. Suspension strut nut
2. End collar
3. Rubber damper
4. Coil spring cap
5. Coil spring
6. Bumper
7. Threaded cap
8. Shock absorber

Exploded view of suspension strut

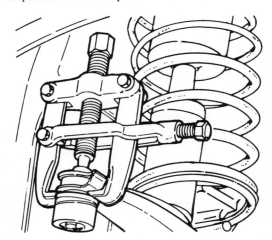

Detaching tie-rod end with puller

5. At the tie-rod end, remove the cotter pin, unscrew the castellated nut, and pull the end off the strut with a puller.

6. Disconnect the end of the stabilizer bar from the strut which is being removed.

Brake caliper retaining bolts and brake line clip (top arrow)

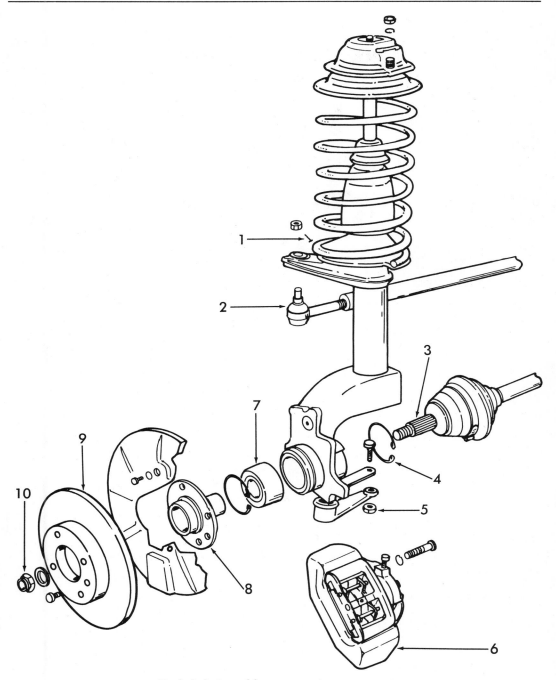

Exploded view of front suspension components

1. Cotter pin
2. Tie-rod
3. Axle driveshaft
4. Circlip
5. Retainer nut
6. Brake caliper
7. Wheel bearing
8. Hub
9. Brake disc
10. Axle nut

7. Remove the ball joint as described in "Ball Joint Removal and Installation."

8. Pull the transaxle driveshaft away from the struct.

9. Remove the upper strut-to-fender retaining nuts.

Upper strut-to-fender retaining nuts

10. Pull the strut assembly down and out of the car.

11. Installation is the reverse of removal. The axle nut is tightened to 138 ft lbs, lower control arm-to-strut 25 ft lbs, caliper-to-strut 43 ft lbs, and stabilizer-to-control arm 7 ft lbs.

COIL SPRING AND SHOCK ABSORBER SERVICE

Due to the necessity of using a spring compressor, these procedures are best left to a dealer or spring shop. To remove the spring, the strut must be mounted in a large vise, the spring compressed, the retaining nut and cover removed, and the spring slowly released. A special tool is needed to remove the shock absorber retainer, after which the shock absorber is easily removed.

LOWER CONTROL ARM

Removal and Installation

1. Raise the front of the car and support it properly.

2. Loosen the upper ball joint retaining bolt and disconnect the ball joint.

3. Remove the stabilizer bar.

4. Remove the control arm retaining bolts that attach the control arm to the frame.

5. Remove the control arm.

6. Installation is the reverse of removal.

FRONT END ALIGNMENT

NOTE: *To ensure proper front end alignment, your car must be taken to a shop that is equipped to handle alignment jobs. The following sections will only tell you what the terms used in front end work mean, not how to actually line up the front end of your Fox.*

Camber Adjustment

Camber is the inward or outward tilt of a steering tire from an imaginary vertical line running through a tire from top to bottom. Positive camber means that the wheel tilts out from this line, while negative camber means that the wheel tilts in from it. Steering axis inclination is closely interrelated with camber, as this is the inward tilt of the steering knuckle from the same imaginary line that was used to determine camber. The combined camber and steering axis inclination angles place the turning point of the front wheel at the center of the tire tread area that's in contact with the road surface. This combination provides easier steering, reduces the load of the outer wheel bearing and improves cornering ability.

The Fox system, called Negative Kingpin Offset, differs from the conventional system described above in that the imaginary vertical line does not fall in the center of the tire tread, but falls outside of the center tire altogether. The benefit of this system is that if a flat tire should occur at speed, the tire instead of turning outward and causing the car to go out of control, is forced to turn back to the straight-ahead path.

A car with a conventional inclination would be pulled to the side, where the Fox is forced to stop in a straight line.

Camber is adjusted by loosening the two ball joint-to-lower control arm bolts, and moving the strut in or out as necessary.

Caster Adjustment

Caster angle uses the weight and force of the car to guide the front wheels in a straight line. It is the number of degrees in which a line drawn through the steering knuckle is inclined from the vertical toward the front or rear of the car. There

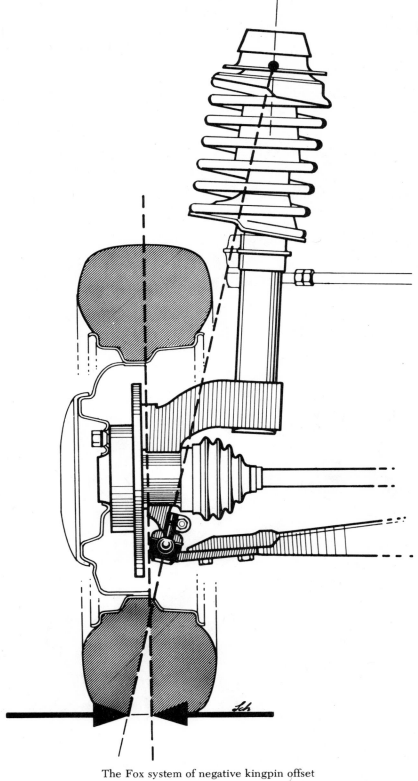

The Fox system of negative kingpin offset

Wheel Alignment (deg)

Caster		Camber			Steering Axis Inclination
Range (deg)	Pref Setting (deg)	Range (deg)	Pref Setting (deg)	Toe-in (deg)	
0° to 1P	0° 30'	0° 5'P to 0° 55'P	0° 30'P	0° 10' ± 10'	——

is no caster adjustment possible on the Fox other than the replacement of parts.

Toe-In

Toe-in is the distance that the front wheels are closer together in front than at the rear, and is usually measured at the wheel hub. Most front wheel drive cars are set with toe-out because the driving wheels have a tendency to toe-in excessively. The Fox front suspension makes a toe-out setting unnecessary.

With the wheels straight-ahead, toe-in is adjusted by loosening the clamps and nuts, and adjusting the length of the tie-rods.

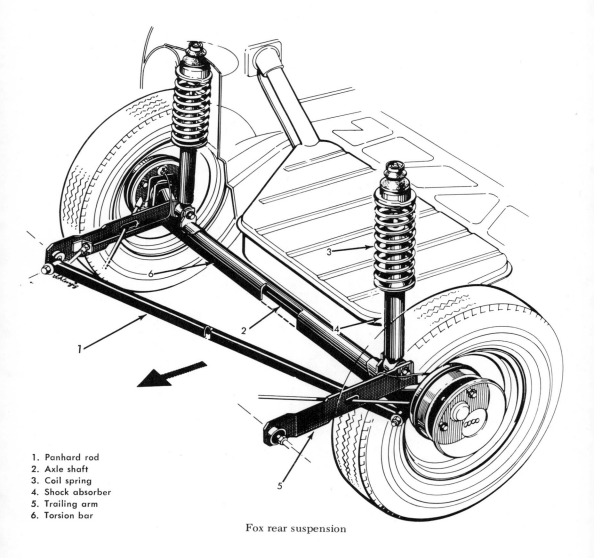

1. Panhard rod
2. Axle shaft
3. Coil spring
4. Shock absorber
5. Trailing arm
6. Torsion bar

Fox rear suspension

Rear Suspension

The rear suspension of the Fox consists of a rear axle containing a full length torsion bar. A trailing arm in front of the axle beam is welded to it, one on each side. The other end of the trailing arm mounts to the body with a rubber bushing. Shock absorbers are located inside the coil-springs and act together with them to provide a smoother ride. A Panhard rod (stabilizer bar) is mounted diagonally between the body and axle to locate the axle against lateral forces.

SHOCK ABSORBERS

Removal and Installation

1. Bend the seat back tabs open from inside the trunk; release the circular locking assemblies.

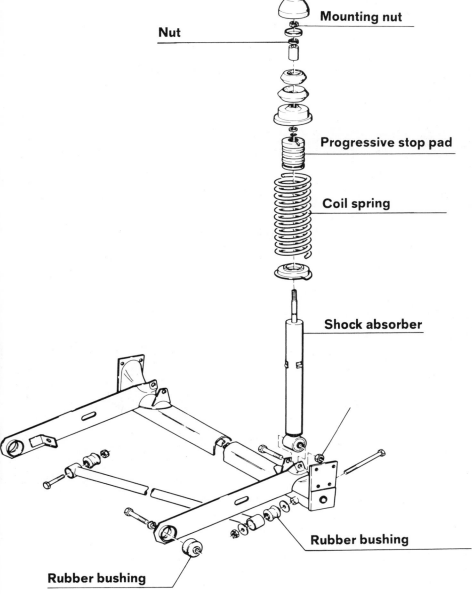

Nut

Mounting nut

Progressive stop pad

Coil spring

Shock absorber

Rubber bushing

Rubber bushing

Fox rear suspension components

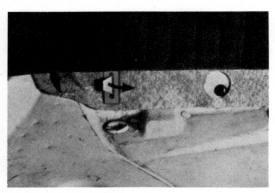

Rear seat locking tabs

2. Pull the backrest forward and remove it from the upper retaining brackets.

3. Remove the cover from the upper shock mount.

4. Remove the upper mounting nut, washer and rubber washer.

Rear shock absorber upper mounting nut

5. Remove the lower mounting bolts and withdraw the coil spring-shock assembly.

NOTE: *When removing the rear shocks on a 1975 Fox, be careful not to damage any of the fuel lines which may be in the way.*

6. Installation is the reverse of removal, but remember to torque the upper mounting bolt to 21 ft lbs and the lower mounting bolt (connected to axle), to 43 ft lbs.

7. To disassemble the coil spring shock unit, loosen the nuts at the top of the shock absorber gradually, one turn of each at a time. Before loosening, the mounting nut should be replaced on the shock as a stop for the slotted nut so that it may be removed safely.

8. Remove all rings and spacers, then remove the snap-rings below the upper spring retainer, and finally remove the stop pad.

9. Assembly is the reverse of disassembly. Make sure that the slotted nut is torqued to 11 ft lbs, and the upper shock mounting bolt to 21 ft lbs. mounting bolt to 21 fit lbs.

Steering

Rack and pinion steering is used on the Fox, with the tie-rods being mounted in the center of the steering rack.

This system allows little toe-in change during suspension travel. A steering damper, like a shock absorber, reduces the road shock that is transmitted to the steering wheel.

The steering geometry is designed to give a variable ratio effect, giving faster steering response as the steering wheel is turned toward either right or left lock. The steering column and linkage is arranged so as to break away and telescope safely in an accident, rather than penetrating into the passenger compartment. The rack and pinion steering system requires no maintenance.

STEERING WHEEL

Removal and Installation

1. Grasp the center cover pad and pull it from the wheel.

2. Loosen and remove the steering shaft nut.

Steering wheel cover pad removed showing horn wire (arrow)

3. Pull the wheel off the shaft.

4. Disconnect the horn wire.

5. Replace the wheel in the reverse order of removal. Tighten the nut to 36 ft lbs.

Drilling out the ignition switch shear bolts

Turn signal switch housing removed from steering column exposing switch electrical connections

TURN SIGNAL SWITCH

1. Disconnect the battery ground cable.

2. Remove the steering wheel.

3. Remove the switch retaining screws.

4. Pry the switch housing off the column.

5. Disconnect the electrical plugs at the back of the switch.

6. Remove the switch housing.

7. Replace in the reverse order of removal.

IGNITION SWITCH AND STEERING LOCK

Removal and Installation

1. Remove the steering wheel and turn signal as outlined above. Remove the steering column shaft covers.

2. The lock is clamped to the steering column with special bolts whose heads shear off on installation. These must be drilled out in order to remove the switch.

3. On replacement, make sure that the lock tang is aligned with the slot in the steering column.

TIE-RODS

Removal and Installation

1. Raise the car and remove the front wheels.

2. Disconnect the outer end of the steering tie-rod from the steering knuckle by removing the cotter pin and nut and pressing out the tie-rod end. A small puller or press is required to free the tie-rod end.

3. Under the hood, pry off the lock plate and remove the mounting bolts from both tie-rod inner ends. Pry the tie-rod out of the mounting pivot.

4. First install the mounting pivot to the rack with both mounting bolts. Remove one bolt, install the tie-rod, and replace the bolt. Do the same on the other tie-rod. Make sure to install the lock plate. The inner tie-rod end bolts should be torqued to 40 ft lbs.

5. If you are replacing the adjustable left tie-rod, adjust it to the same length as the old one. Check the toe-in when the job is done.

6. Use new cotter pins when installing the outer tie-rod ends. Torque the nut to 28 ft lbs.

Chapter Eight

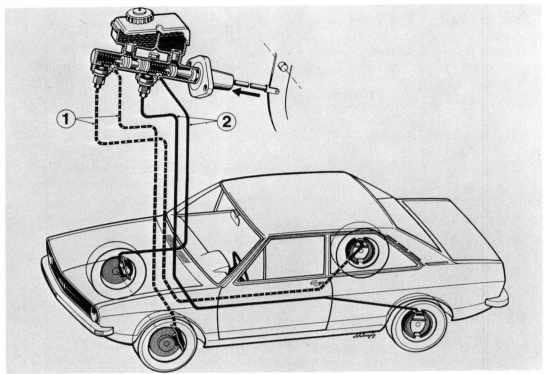

Brakes

Brake System

Brakes are a balanced set of mechanical devices used on each wheel to convert the mechanical energy of your car into another form of energy. Brakes convert the forward motion of your car into heat energy by the friction caused by their rubbing on the brake disc or drum. This is accomplished by the rubbing of the brake pad in front and the brake shoe in the rear, on the disc and drum.

The friction that results from these elements coming in contact with each other slows the car down. Each time that you step on the brakes, you're starting this process by creating hydraulic pressure in the brake lines which forces the brake components to contact each other and creat friction, thus transferring one form of energy into another.

The conversion process of mechanical energy to heat energy is not the end however; some way must be found to dissipate the heat energy since the heat generated by braking is often far in excess of the amount that the components can handle. The heat that is built up is removed by the air circulating around the brake, and the length of time between brake applications. Since brake application time cannot be designed into a brake, more effective air cooling is one way to more effective braking. This has led to the popularity of the disc brake with its more effective cooling. Your Fox uses disc brakes at the front with drum brakes at the rear.

Drum brakes, while not as effective at heat dissipation, provide a better means of securing the car while it is parked. The combination of disc brakes at the front and drum brakes at the rear has proved to be a very popular combination since it provides good braking under all situations encountered in normal driving.

ADJUSTMENT

The front disc brake requires no adjustment because the disc brakes automatically adjust themselves to compensate for pad wear. The rear drum brakes must be periodically adjusted, once or twice a year depending on condition.

1. Raise the rear of the car. Place a jack under the center of the torsion bar-axle. The jack pad should be at least 4 in. square, otherwise you might damage the axle.

2. Block the front wheels and release the parking brake. Step on the brake pedal hard to center the linings.

Rear brake adjusting nuts

a. Turning the nut clockwise tightens the brake shoe against the drum.
b. Turning the nut counterclockwise will allow the wheel to turn freely.

3. Turn the front adjusting nut on the brake backing plate until the wheel can't be rotated by hand.

4. Loosen the adjusting nut until the wheel can be turned freely without drag.

5. Repeat Steps 3 and 4 for the rear adjusting nut on the brake backing plate.

6. Repeat Steps 3, 4, and 5 for the opposite wheel.

7. Step on the brake pedal hard a few times to make sure that the wheels spin without dragging.

Hydraulic System

The Fox hydraulic system is a dual circuit type which has the advantage of retaining 50% braking effectiveness in the event of failure in one system. The circuits are arranged so that you always have one front and one rear brake for a more controlled emergency stop. The right front and left rear are one circuit; the left front and right rear are the second circuit. The dual master cylinder is at-

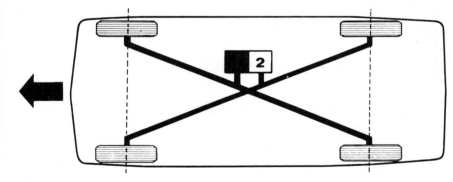

Dual hydraulic circuit

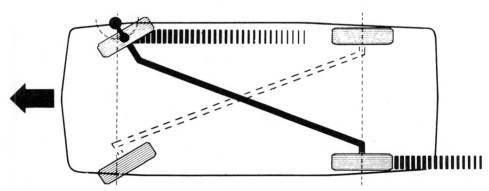

One front and rear brake remain operational when one system fails

Master cylinder and vacuum booster unit

tached to the brake booster which is in turn bolted to the firewall. The booster uses intake manifold vacuum to provide a pedal assist. This booster is used because disc brakes generally require more pedal effort than drum brakes.

The brake pedal assembly is linked to the master cylinder by a pushrod and yoke. Since the brake fluid cannot be compressed, as liquids are not compressible, stepping on the brake pedal causes the master cylinder pistons to transmit hydraulic pressure to the brake unit at each wheel. This pressure is transmitted through the brake lines. In addition to the master cylinder, brake lines, and wheel cylinders, the Fox has a brake failure switch and a proportioning valve.

The brake failure unit is a hydraulic valve/eletrical switch which will alert you of brake problems via the warning light on the dashboard. A piston inside the switch is kept centered by one brake system's pressure on one side, and the other system's pressure on the opposite side. Should a failure occur in one system, the piston would move to the "bad" side and complete the electrical circuit to the warning lamp. This switch also functions as a parking brake "engaged" reminder light and will go out when the brake is released.

The proportioning valve, actually two separate valves on manual transmission sedans, provides balanced front-to-rear braking during hard stops. A panic stop shifts a larger percentage of the car's weight to the front, which in turn causes the rear brakes to lock. The front disc brakes also require more operating pressure than the rear drums so the situation is compounded. Extreme brake line pressure will overcome the spring pressure on the piston within the valve and it proportionally restricts pressure to the rear brakes. In this manner, the rear brakes are kept from locking up. The proportioner doesn't work under normal braking conditions.

MASTER CYLINDER

Removal and Installation

1. Place a protective cover over the car's fender to protect it from any brake fluid which may accidentally spill.

2. Disconnect and plug the brake lines.

3. Remove the terminal connectors

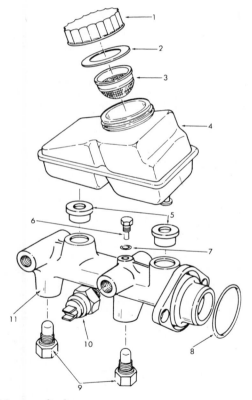

Master cylinder

1. Reservoir cap
2. Washer
3. Filter screen
4. Reservoir
5. Master cylinder plugs
6. Stop screw
7. Stop screw seal
8. Master cylinder seal
9. Residual pressure valves
10. Warning light sender unit
11. Brake master cylinder housing

from the sending unit of the brake failure switch.

4. Remove the master cylinder mounting nuts and remove the master cylinder from the brake booster. Be careful not to spill any fluid on the car's paint. Empty the fluid from the reservoir and discard it.

CAUTION: *Do not depress the brake pedal while the master cylinder is removed.*

5. Place the master cylinder on the booster studs and install the washers and nuts. Tighten the nuts to no more than 10 ft lbs.

6. Remove the plugs one at a time and reconnect the brake lines.

7. Bleed the entire brake system as outlined later on in this chapter.

Overhaul

Purchase the proper overhaul kit for your car and enough brake fluid before starting the procedure. Two small cans should be more than enough.

1. Remove the master cylinder from the booster.

2. Mount the master cylinder in vise using clean rags to protect the sides of the cylinder that come in contact with the vise.

3. Pull the plastic master cylinder reservoir out of the rubber plugs, and remove the plugs.

4. Remove the stop screw from the center of the cylinder. You may throw away the stop screw gasket as a new one is included in the overhaul kit.

5. With a pair of snap-ring pliers, remove the snap-ring (circlip) from the end of the master cylinder.

6. Shake out the secondary piston assembly. If the primary piston remains lodged in the bore, it can be forced out by applying compressed air to the open brake line fitting.

7. Take the secondary piston apart. The two secondary rings will be replaced with ones from the rebuilding kit, but keep the washers and spacers.

8. Carefully clamp the secondary piston, slightly compress the spring, and unscrew the stroke limiting bolt.

9. Remove the secondary piston stop sleeve bolt, spring, spring seat, and support washer.

10. Replace the parts of the master cyl-

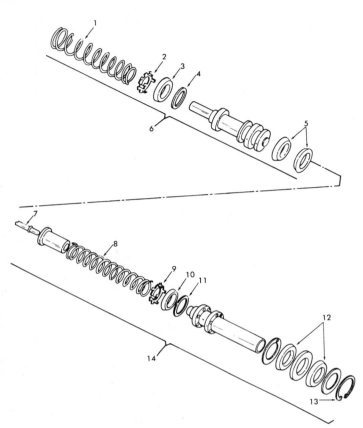

1. Conical spring
2. Spring seat
3. Primary cup
4. Washer
5. Secondary cups
6. Primary piston assembly
7. Stroke limiting screw
8. Cylindrical spring
9. Spring seat
10. Primary cup
11. Washer
12. Secondary cups
13. Circlip
14. Secondary piston assembly

Exploded view of master cylinder components

inder with those supplied in the overhaul kit.

11. Clean all the metal parts in a suitable solvent such as denatured alcohol, and dry them.

12. Check all the parts that are being reused carefully. Pay close attention to the cylinder bores; if there is any scoring or rust, have the master cylinder honed or replace it. Discard any parts which show signs of fatigue.

13. Lightly coat the bores and cups with brake fluid. Assemble the components in the exact sequence shown in the illustration.

14. Install the primary piston assembly, notice that the primary spring is conically shaped. Make sure that you aren't using the secondary spring.

15. Using a plastic rod, or other non-metallic tool, push the primary piston assembly into the housing until the stop bolt (with a new seal), can be screwed in and tightened.

16. Assemble the secondary piston.

Fasten the spring, spring seat, primary cup, and stop sleeve to the piston with the stroke limiting bolt.

17. Assemble the remaining master cylinder components in the reverse order of disassembly. Ensure that the snap-ring is fully seated and that the piston cups are properly positioned.

18. Install and tighten the brake failure warning sending unit.

BRAKE PRESSURE REGULATOR VALVE

Manual transaxle equipped Foxes are equipped with two brake pressure regulator valves mounted under the master cylinder on a bracket attached to the brake booster. These valves are not repairable, and must be replaced when found to be defective. A simple check will determine their condition.

With an assistant holding down the brake pedal, place your hand on the valves; then, have him release the pedal. If the valves are working, you should feel a slight knock in both valves as the pistons return. If you suspect that the valves are bad, from either this test, a "soft" brake pedal, or the car's tendency to pull to one side when braking, take the car to a dealer to have it checked, as they have the pressure gauges necessary to perform a complete test. There is also a pressure regulator for the rear wheels located on the right rear of 1975 models, next to the axle.

BLEEDING

Anytime a brake line has been disconnected, the hydraulic system should be bled. The brakes should also be bled if you notice your brake pedal becoming soft or the car pulls to one side when you apply the brakes. The system is bled from the wheels, the proper sequence being: right rear wheel, left rear wheel, right front caliper, and left front caliper. An assistant is necessary to pump the brake pedal while you open the bleeder valves.

If the system has been drained, refill it with new brake fluid. Using the preceding wheel sequence, open each bleeder valve ½ to ¾ of a turn and pump the brake pedal until fluid flows out of the valve. When you've finished, proceed with the steps outlined below.

1. Remove the bleeder valve dust cover from the wheel you're working on, and place a rubber bleeder hose over the end of the bleeder valve.

2. Insert the other end of the hose into a container about ½ full of brake fluid. Make sure that this container is clean before using it.

3. Have your assistant pump the brake pedal several times until the pressure increases in the pedal.

4. Hold the pedal under pressure and then start to open the bleeder valve about ½ to ¾ of a turn. At this point, have your assistant depress the pedal all the way and then quickly close the valve. The assistant should release his foot slowly from the pedal, letting it rise in a slow, even motion.

NOTE: *Keep checking the fluid level in the master cylinder and top it up as necessary in the bleeding process.*

5. Keep repeating this process until no more air bubbles can be seen coming from the hose in the can of brake fluid. You may have to repeat Step 4 three to four times bevore all the air is out of the system.

6. Remove the bleeder hose and install the dust cover.

7. Move to the next wheel in sequence and bleed that one.

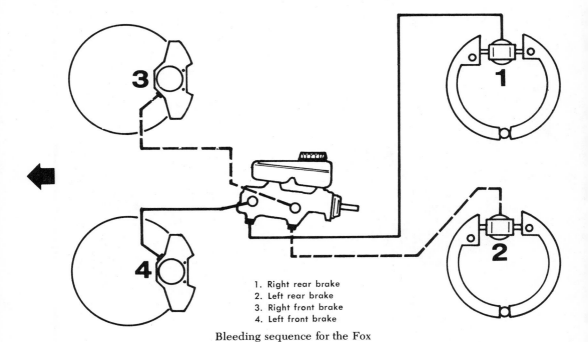

1. Right rear brake
2. Left rear brake
3. Right front brake
4. Left front brake

Bleeding sequence for the Fox

Bleeder valve with cap installed (top arrow) and brake adjusting screws (bottom arrows)

Make sure that when you're bleeding the wheels, the car is adequately supported if you've jacked it up to bleed the wheels. Also, don't get any brake fluid on the paint as the ingredients in the brake fluid will mar the paint. If any comes in contact with the paint, immediately wash it off with water.

Front Disc Brakes

The Fox uses single-piston, floating caliper disc brakes on the front wheels. As the hydraulic pressure forces one pad against the rotating brake disc, counter pressure forces the floating frame to press the other pad against the disc.

BRAKE PADS

Removal and Installation

Brake pads should be replaced when there is no visible clearance between the pads and the cross-spring, or when the pads are worn to a thickness of 0.08 in. Before starting this operation, siphon out about half of the brake fluid in the master cylinder to prevent it from overflowing when the piston is pushed in and the new thicker brake pads are installed.

NOTE: *1975 Foxes have brake pad wear indicators built into the pads. When the pad wears down to the point where replacement is necessary, the brake pedal will pulsate when the brakes are applied. Removal and installation procedures for these pads are the same as those for the older pads.*

1. Jack up the car and support it

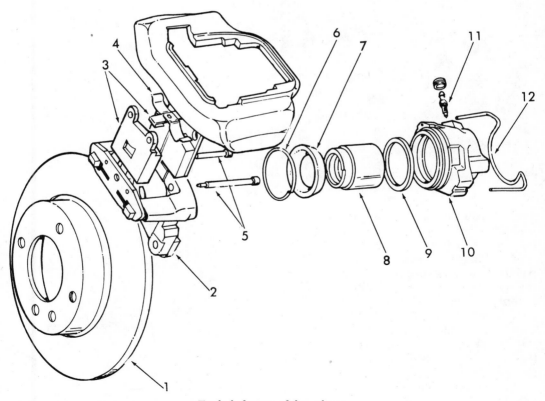

Exploded view of the caliper

1. Brake disc
2. Caliper mounting frame
3. Pads
4. Cross spring
5. Retaining pins
6. Clamp irng
7. Boot
8. Piston
9. Seal
10. Cylinder
11. Bleeder nipple
12. Guide spring

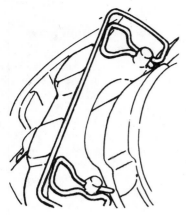

Retaining clip

safely on stands, then remove the front wheels.

2. Pry the retaining clip out of both retaining pins.

Removing the brake pad retaining pins
a. Break-off element

3. While pressing down on the cross-spring, tap the brake pad retaining pins out with a drift or small screwdriver.

4. Make reference marks on the brake pads if you are going to reuse them, then remove the cross-spring and break-off element.

5. Remove the inner brake pad. Audi uses a special tool for this purpose, P-86, but by using a small drift you can pry the pad out of the caliper until it can be gripped by a pair of pliers and removed.

6. The outer brake pad is positioned in a notch. A flat, smooth piece of hardwood or metal should be used to press the caliper frame and piston cylinder outward so the pad can be released from its notch and then removed.

Removing the outer disc brake pad

7. Grip the outer pad and remove it. Press the piston back into the cylinder with the tool used in Step 6.

8. Check that the piston is at the proper 20° angle. This can be done by making a gauge out of stiff cardboard or by using Audi tool, P-84.

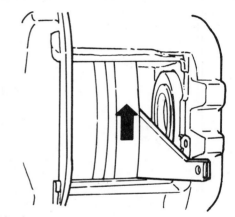

Checking piston positioning

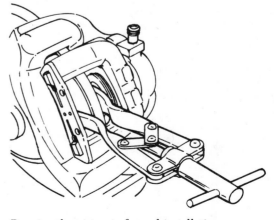

Pressing the piston in for pad installation

9. Install the brake pads into the caliper. If the old pads are being reused, replace them in the side of the caliper

from which they were removed. When installing new pads, always replace them in both wheels at the same time.

10. Position the cross-spring and break-off element in the caliper and then carefully tap the pad retaining pins into place with a small hammer. Install the re-taining pin.

CALIPERS

Removal and Installation

1. Jack up the front of the car and support it on stands.

2. Disconnect and plug the brake line. This is not necessary if the caliper is not being taken off the car. If it is being left on the car, hang it out of the way.

3. Remove the two caliper-to-strut retaining bolts and remove the caliper.

4. Install the caliper using the reverse of the removal procedure. The two caliper retaining bolts are torqued to 43 ft lbs.

5. If the brake line has been disconnected, bleed the brakes.

Overhaul

Before you begin this procedure, make sure that you have the proper rebuilding kit, solvents, and enough brake fluid to complete the job.

1. Remove the caliper and brake pads.

2. Place the caliper in a soft jawed vise, or wrap the jaws of a vise with a cloth to protect the caliper.

3. Pry the fixed mounting frame off the floating frame.

4. Separate the caliper cylinder from the floating frame by prying it and the

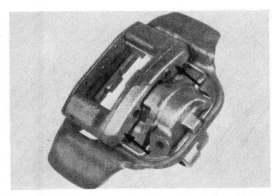
Removing the mounting frame from the floating frame

Separating the caliper cylinder from the floating frame

Removing the piston clamp ring from the caliper cylinder

guide spring off the frame. Use a soft drift (such as brass), to lightly tap on the cylinder and place a piece of wood under the piston to protect it.

5. Using pliers, remove the piston clamp ring. Remove and discard the dust cover.

6. Remove the piston from the cylinder. If it is stubborn, remove the bleeder screw and blow it out with compressed air.

CAUTION: *Hold the piston over a block of wood when doing this because the piston will fly out with considerable force.*

7. After the piston comes out of the caliper, remove the rubber seal with a plastic or wood pin. Be careful not to damage the seal groove.

8. Once disassembled, all the metal parts should be cleaned in denatured alcohol. Never use mineral based solvents such as gasoline or kerosene, as these will weaken rubber parts. The pistons and their bores should be inspected at this time. They should be free of scoring

and pitting; if there is any visible damage, replace the part.

9. Discard all the rubber parts as they are included in the rebuilding kit.

10. Lightly coat the cylinder bore, piston and seal with clean brake fluid.

11. Install the piston into the cylinder using a vise.

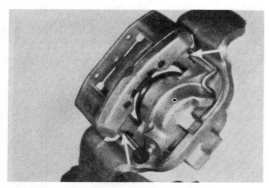

The guide spring in place in the groove of the brake cylinder

12. Place the guide spring in the groove of the brake cylinder, and using a brass drift, install the cylinder on the floating frame.

The mounting frame in position on the floating frame

13. Place the mounting frame in the guide spring and slip it onto the floating frame. The fixed frame has two grooves which position it over the raised ribs of the floating frame.

14. Install the pads, caliper and bleed the brakes.

BRAKE DISC

Inspection and Checking

Brake discs may be checked for lateral run-out while installed on the car. This check will require a dial indicator gauge and stand to mount it on the caliper. Audi

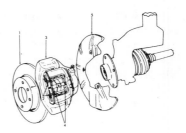

1. Brake disc	4. Brake pads
2. Retaining pins	5. Splash shield
3. Brake caliper	

Caliper and disc mounting

has a special tool for this purpose which mounts the dial indicator to the caliper, but it can also be mounted on the shaft of a C-clamp attached to the outside of the caliper.

1. Remove the wheel and reinstall the wheel bolts (torqued to 58 ft lbs) to retain the disc to the hub.

2. Mount the dial indicator securely to the caliper. The feeler should touch about ½ in. below the outer edge.

3. Rotate the disc and observe the gauge. Radial run-out (wobble) must not exceed 0.004 in. (0.1 mm). A disc which exceeds this specification must be replaced or refinished.

4. Brake discs which have excessive radial run-out, sharp ridges, or scoring can be refinished. First grinding must be done on both sides of the disc to prevent squeaking and vibrating. Discs which have only light grooves and are otherwise acceptable can be used without refinishing.

5. The standard disc is 0.47 in. (12 mm) thick. It should not be ground to less than 0.39 in. (11 mm).

Removal and Installation

1. Loosen the wheel lug bolts, jack up the front of the car and support it safely on stands; and then remove the wheels.

2. Remove the caliper as outlined elsewhere in this chapter.

3. Remove the disc to hub retaining screw.

4. Grip the disc and pull it off. If it is hard to remove, use a puller on it, never hammer on it.

5. The disc is installed in the reverse order of removal. Make sure that you bleed the brakes when finished, and torque the wheel lug bolts to 58 ft lbs.

1. Grease cap
2. Nut
3. Wheel bearing
4. Brake drum
5. Cotter pin
6. Eccentrics
7. Return spring
8. Adjuster
9. Retaining spring
10. Brake shoe

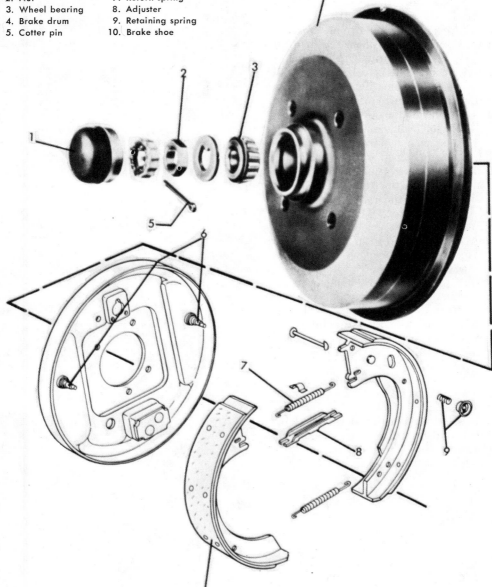

Exploded view of the rear brake

Rear Drum Brakes

1. Loosen the wheel lug bolts, raise and safely support the car, and remove the wheels.

2. Pry off the grease cap, and remove and discard the cotter pin.

3. Remove both the castellated and hex nuts along with the washer.

4. Pull off the brake drum. Be careful not to lose the inner race of the outer bearing. If the brake drum is stubborn, remove the rubber cover on the baking plate and back off the brake adjuster with an adjusting tool or wide-bladed screw-driver. If this doesn't work, use a puller,

but under no circumstances should you use heat or hammer on the brake drum.

5. Check the brake drum for any cracks, scores, grooves or an out-of-roundness condition. Replace the drum if it shows signs of scoring. Light scoring can be smoothed with sandpaper, but if extensive, you should have the drum turned down. The drum should never be turned down more than 0.03 in.

6. The axle bearings in the brake drum must be pressed out for replacement. A machine shop can handle this operation, but when reinstalling, make sure that new seals are used. The outer bearing is retained by a circlip on early models, but as of chassis number 8232-055-852 (automatic trans.) and 8232-067-397 manual trans.), no circlip is used. It was replaced by a collar in the drum itself.

7. After greasing the bearings and installing them in the hub with new seals, place the drum on the stub axle.

8. Install the washer and hex nut. Tighten the nut and then loosen it. Retighten the nut slightly so that the washer between the nut and the bearing can just be moved with a screwdriver. Correct bearing play is 0.0012-0.0027 in. (0.03-0.07 mm).

9. Install the castellated nut and insert a new cotter pin. Fill the hub dust cover with grease and install it.

10. Install the wheel and lower the car.

BRAKE SHOES

Removal and Installation

1. Remove the brake drum.

2. Using brake pliers, disconnect the lower spring.

3. Disconnect the anchor spring and pins from each shoe. You can do this with a pair of pliers, but there is a brake tool available at most auto supply stores that will make the job much easier.

4. Lift up on the brake shoes and detach the parking brake cable by pressing back the spring with needlenose pliers and then disconnecting the cable at the lever. Remove the brake shoes and spreader bar.

5. Clean and inspect all brake parts. There are spray solvents available for

Disconnecting the lower brake spring with pliers

Disconnecting the anchor spring and pin from the rear brake shoe

Detaching the parking brake cable

brake cleaning which will not affect the brake lining, but be careful not to get the solvent on the rubber parts.

6. Check the wheel cylinders for cup condition and wear.

7. Inspect the replacement shoes for nicks or burrs. Lubricate the backing plate contact points, the brake cable, and lever with Lubriplate®.

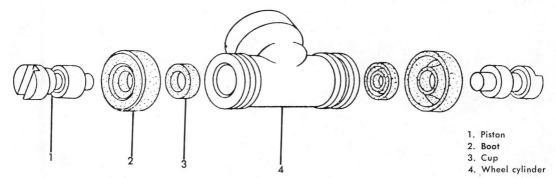

1. Piston
2. Boot
3. Cup
4. Wheel cylinder

Exploded view of the rear wheel cylinder

8. Reverse the removal procedure for assembly. When completed, install the drum and adjust the rear brakes as shown elsewhere in this chapter.

WHEEL CYLINDERS

Removal and Installation

1. Remove the brake drums and shoes.
2. Depress the brake pedal about two in. to block the master cylinder compensating port and prevent leakage. Support the pedal in this position.
3. Remove the brake line and plug it, making sure that the line is not damaged when pulled away from the wheel.
4. Remove the bolts and lockwashers that attach the wheel cylinder to the brake backing plate, and remove the cylinder.
5. Installation is the reverse of the removal process.

Overhaul

1. Remove the brakes.
2. Fluid will run out of the cylinder when it's taken apart, so make sure that you have something underneath the brake to catch the fluid.
3. Remove the rubber boots from the ends of the cylinder.
4. Push one piston toward the center of the cylinder to force the opposite piston and cup out the other end of the cylinder. When finished, reach in the open end and push the other side's spring, cup, and piston out.
5. Remove the bleeder screw from the rear of the cylinder, on the back of the brake backing plate.
6. Inspect the inside of the wheel cylinder. If scored in any way, it must be honed with a wheel cylinder hone or

crocus cloth. If it is excessively worn (more than 0.003 in.), the cylinder should be replaced. Whenever honing or cleaning a wheel cylinder, make sure that you keep a small amount of brake fluid in the cylinder as lubricant.

7. Clean any foreign matter from the pistons, and when finished, run a clean cloth through it to remove all traces of foreign matter.
8. Install the bleeder screw and return screw in the piston.
9. Coat the new cylinder cups with clean brake fluid and install them in the cylinder. Make certain that they are square in the bore or they'll leak.
10. Install the pistons in the cylinder after coating them with new brake fluid.
11. Coat the insides of the boots with new brake fluid and install them on the cylinder. Install and bleed the brakes.

Parking Brake

The parking brake on the Fox is a standard design, being a rod attached to the

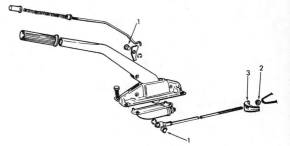

Parking brake handle assembly
1. Retaining pin
2. Parking brake adjusting nut
3. Cable compensator

Parking brake cable compensator location

brake lever which when pulled, activates the rear brakes through a compensater and cable to each brake drum.

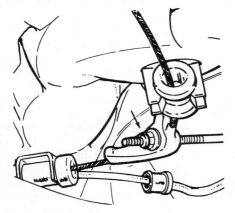

Parking brake adjusting nut

CABLE

Adjustment

Parking brake adjustment is made at the cable compensater, attached to the parking brake lever pushrod.

1. Block the front wheels and jack to the rear of the car high enough for you to work under.

2. Pull the parking brake lever up two notches.

3. From under the car, tighten the compensator nut until the rear wheels can just be turned by hand.

4. Release the brake lever and check that both wheels turn easily.

5. Lubricate the compensator with grease.

Brake Specifications

All measurements are given in inches (mm)

Master Cylinder Bore	Wheel Cylinder Bore		Brake Disc or Drum Diameter	
	Front	Rear	Front	Rear
0.82 (20.64)	1.73 (44)	NA	9.41 (239)	7.87 (200)

NA Not available

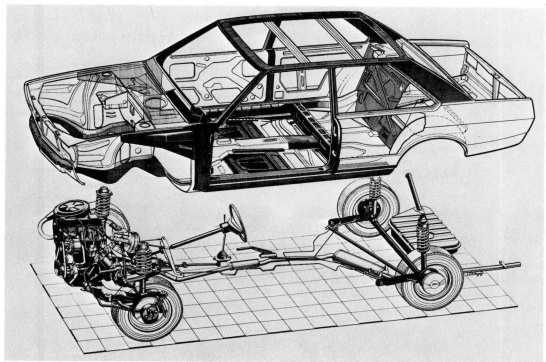

Chapter Nine

Body

Doors

Removal and Installation

1. Remove the door panel.
2. Mark the position of the hinges on the door if the door is to be reused.
3. Remove the door limiting strap by driving out the tensioning pin after removing the circlip.
4. While supporting the door, remove the retaining bolt and remove the door.
5. To remove the hinges, remove the side panels to gain access, and remove the retaining bolts.
6. Installation is the reverse of removal.

DOOR PANELS

Removal and Installation

1. Pry the window crank trim button off the window crank.
2. Remove the screw underneath and remove the crank.

3. Remove the arm rest retaining screws, and unscrew the lock button.
4. Pry off the door panel with a putty knife and remove it by pulling up and off. When prying it off, use the knife close to the clips to avoid damage.
5. Installation is the reverse of removal.

DOOR HANDLE AND LOCK

Removal and Installation

1. Remove the phillips screws on the edge of the door.
2. Push the door handle slightly forward and remove it.
3. Remove the door panel.
4. Remove the lock mounting screws from the edge of the door.
5. Pry off the linkage retaining clip and separate the linkage from the lock mechanism.
6. Remove the remote control lever and disconnect the linkage.
7. Remove the lock through the access hole in the door.

Door lock mounting screws

8. Installation is the reverse of removal, but before reinstalling the door panel, make sure that the plastic weather protection sheet is glued properly back in place.

Window Adjustment

There is no window adjustment possible, but if the windows are hard to operate, remove the door panel and lubricate the crank mechanism.

Hood and Trunk

Alignment

The hood and trunk can be aligned by loosening the hinge bolts in their slotted mounting holes and moving the hood or trunk lid as necessary. The catches are also adjustable in the same manner to provide easy engagement.

Remote Control Mirror

Removal and Installation

All 1975 Foxes are equipped with outside remote control rear view mirrors. To remove them:

1. Pry off the inside trim cap.
2. Remove the phillips head screw and pull the knob off the shaft.

3. From the outside, remove the base cover plate.
4. Remove the screws and remove the mirror.
5. Installation is the reverse of removal but it may be helpful to remove the door trim panel to gain greater access when installing the mirror.

Fuel Tank

Removal and Installation

CAUTION: *When following any procedure that involves the fuel system, be extremely careful of fire. Make sure that there are no possible items around that could ignite fuel vapors and cause a fire.*

1. Disconnect the battery ground cable.
2. Remove the trunk floor mat. Drain the fuel tank.
3. Disconnect the fuel line.
4. Remove the electrical plugs from the tank sending unit.
5. Remove the vent line.
6. Remove the tank retaining bolts and remove the filler tube from the tank.
7. Remove the tank.
8. Installation is the reverse of removal, but make sure that you reseal the lower edge of the trunk floor to prevent leaks.

Dashboard

Removal and Installation

1. Remove the three retaining screws on the driver's side lower fascia panel.
2. Remove the ash tray and remove the four retaining screws on the right-side.
NOTE: *On these retaining screws, when unscrewed, slide them down and forward to remove them completely.*
3. Remove the dash mounting nuts in the engine compartment. They are accessible through the water drain box.

Dash retaining springs (arrows) and multipole connecter plug terminals (circles)

4. Remove all plugs, knobs, and air tubes.

5. Remove the speedometer cable from its connection on the dash. Remove the multipole connector from the back of the instrument panel and unhook the panel retaining springs.

6. Remove the dashboard.

7. Installation is the reverse of removal.

Disabling the Seatbelt Interlock System

A change in the Federal law requiring seatbelt interlocks has made them no longer mandatory, allowing you to disconnect the interlock and buzzer, but you must not disconnect the warning light. The procedure that Audi recommends will disable the interlock, but not the buzzer and light since they are interconnected within the same relay.

1. Disconnect the battery ground cable.

2. Find the two heavy gauge wires leading into the logic relay socket to terminals C and 50.

3. About four in. from the socket, strip some insulation from each wire and join them using a heavy wire.

4. Seal the connection with tape and reconnect the battery.

Appendix

General Conversion Table

Multiply by	To convert	To	
2.54	Inches	Centimeters	.3937
30.48	Feet	Centimeters	.0328
.914	Yards	Meters	1.094
1.609	Miles	Kilometers	.621
.645	Square inches	Square cm.	.155
.836	Square yards	Square meters	1.196
16.39	Cubic inches	Cubic cm.	.061
28.3	Cubic feet	Liters	.0353
.4536	Pounds	Kilograms	2.2045
4.546	Gallons	Liters	.22
.068	Lbs./sq. in. (psi)	Atmospheres	14.7
.138	Foot pounds	Kg. m.	7.23
1.014	H.P. (DIN)	H.P. (SAE)	.9861
——	To obtain	From	Multiply by

Note: 1 cm. equals 10 mm.; 1 mm. equals .0394".

Conversion—Common Fractions to Decimals and Millimeters

INCHES			INCHES			INCHES		
Common Fractions	Decimal Fractions	Millimeters (approx.)	Common Fractions	Decimal Fractions	Millimeters (approx.)	Common Fractions	Decimal Fractions	Millimeters (approx.)
1/128	.008	0.20	11/32	.344	8.73	43/64	.672	17.07
1/64	.016	0.40	23/64	.359	9.13	11/16	.688	17.46
1/32	.031	0.79	3/8	.375	9.53	45/64	.703	17.86
3/64	.047	1.19	25/64	.391	9.92	23/32	.719	18.26
1/16	.063	1.59	13/32	.406	10.32	47/64	.734	18.65
5/64	.078	1.98	27/64	.422	10.72	3/4	.750	19.05
3/32	.094	2.38	7/16	.438	11.11	49/64	.766	19.45
7/64	.109	2.78	29/64	.453	11.51	25/32	.781	19.84
1/8	.125	3.18	15/32	.469	11.91	51/64	.797	20.24
9/64	.141	3.57	31/64	.484	12.30	13/16	.813	20.64˙
5/32	.156	3.97	1/2	.500	12.70	53/64	.828	21.03
11/64	.172	4.37	33/64	.516	13.10	27/32	.844	21.43
3/16	.188	4.76	17/32	.531	13.49	55/64	.859	21.83
13/64	.203	5.16	35/64	.547	13.89	7/8	.875	22.23
7/32	.219	5.56	9/16	.563	14.29	57/64	.891	22.62
15/64	.234	5.95	37/64	.578	14.68	29/32	.906	23.02
1/4	.250	6.35	19/32	.594	15.08	59/64	.922	23.42
17/64	.266	6.75	39/64	.609	15.48	15/16	.938	23.81
9/32	.281	7.14	5/8	.625	15.88	61/64	.953	24.21
19/64	.297	7.54	41/64	.641	16.27	31/32	.969	24.61
5/16	.313	7.94	21/32	.656	16.67	63/64	.984	25.00
21/64	.328	8.33						

Conversion—Millimeters to Decimal Inches

mm	inches	mm	inches	mm	inches	mm	inches	mm	inches
1	.039 370	31	1.220 470	61	2.401 570	91	3.582 670	210	8.267 700
2	.078 740	32	1.259 840	62	2.440 940	92	3.622 040	220	8.661 400
3	.118 110	33	1.299 210	63	2.480 310	93	3.661 410	230	9.055 100
4	.157 480	34	1.338 580	64	2.519 680	94	3.700 780	240	9.448 800
5	.196 850	35	1.377 949	65	2.559 050	95	3.740 150	250	9.842 500
6	.236 220	36	1.417 319	66	2.598 420	96	3.779 520	260	10.236 200
7	.275 590	37	1.456 689	67	2.637 790	97	3.818 890	270	10.629 900
8	.314 960	38	1.496 050	68	2.677 160	98	3.858 260	280	11.032 600
9	.354 330	39	1.535 430	69	2.716 530	99	3.897 630	290	11.417 300
10	.393 700	40	1.574 800	70	2.755 900	100	3.937 000	300	11.811 000
11	.433 070	41	1.614 170	71	2.795 270	105	4.133 848	310	12.204 700
12	.472 440	42	1.653 540	72	2.834 640	110	4.330 700	320	12.598 400
13	.511 810	43	1.692 910	73	2.874 010	115	4.527 550	330	12.992 100
14	.551 180	44	1.732 280	74	2.913 380	120	4.724 400	340	13.385 800
15	.590 550	45	1.771 650	75	2.952 750	125	4.921 250	350	13.779 500
16	.629 920	46	1.811 020	76	2.992 120	130	5.118 100	360	14.173 200
17	.669 290	47	1.850 390	77	3.031 490	135	5.314 950	370	14.566 900
18	.708 660	48	1.889 760	78	3.070 860	140	5.511 800	380	14.960 600
19	.748 030	49	1.929 130	79	3.110 230	145	5.708 650	390	15.354 300
20	.787 400	50	1.968 500	80	3.149 600	150	5.905 500	400	15.748 000
21	.826 770	51	2.007 870	81	3.188 970	155	6.102 350	500	19.685 000
22	.866 140	52	2.047 240	82	3.228 340	160	6.299 200	600	23.622 000
23	.905 510	53	2.086 610	83	3.267 710	165	6.496 050	700	27.559 000
24	.944 880	54	2.125 980	84	3.307 080	170	6.692 900	800	31.496 000
25	.984 250	55	2.165 350	85	3.346 450	175	6.889 750	900	35.433 000
26	1.023 620	56	2.204 720	86	3.385 820	180	7.086 600	1000	39.370 000
27	1.062 990	57	2.244 090	87	3.425 190	185	7.283 450	2000	78.740 000
28	1.102 360	58	2.283 460	88	3.464 560	190	7.480 300	3000	118.110 000
29	1.141 730	59	2.322 830	89	3.503 903	195	7.677 150	4000	157.480 000
30	1.181 100	60	2.362 200	90	3.543 300	200	7.874 000	5000	196.850 000

To change decimal millimeters to decimal inches, position the decimal point where desired on either side of the millimeter measurement shown and reset the inches decimal by the same number of digits in the same direction. For example, to convert 0.001 mm into decimal inches, reset the decimal behind the 1 mm (shown on the chart) to 0.001; change the decimal inch equivalent (0.039″ shown) to 0.000039″.

Tap Drill Sizes

	National Fine or S.A.E.				National Coarse or U.S.S.	
Screw & Tap Size	Threads Per Inch	Use Drill Number		Screw & Tap Size	Threads Per Inch	Use Drill Number
No. 5	44	37		No. 5	40	39
No. 6	40	33		No. 6	32	36
No. 8	36	29		No. 8	32	29
No. 10	32	21		No. 10	24	25
No. 12	28	15		No. 12	24	17
$\frac{1}{4}$	28	3		$\frac{1}{4}$	20	8
$\frac{5}{16}$	24	1		$\frac{5}{16}$	18	F
$\frac{3}{8}$	24	Q		$\frac{3}{8}$	16	$\frac{5}{16}$
$\frac{7}{16}$	20	W		$\frac{7}{16}$	14	U
$\frac{1}{2}$	20	$\frac{29}{64}$		$\frac{1}{2}$	13	$\frac{27}{64}$
$\frac{9}{16}$	18	$\frac{33}{64}$		$\frac{9}{16}$	12	$\frac{31}{64}$
$\frac{5}{8}$	18	$\frac{37}{64}$		$\frac{5}{8}$	11	$\frac{17}{32}$
$\frac{3}{4}$	16	$\frac{11}{16}$		$\frac{3}{4}$	10	$\frac{21}{32}$
$\frac{7}{8}$	14	$\frac{13}{16}$		$\frac{7}{8}$	9	$\frac{49}{64}$
$1\frac{1}{8}$	12	$1\frac{3}{64}$		1	8	$\frac{7}{8}$
$1\frac{1}{4}$	12	$1\frac{11}{64}$		$1\frac{1}{8}$	7	$\frac{63}{64}$
$1\frac{1}{2}$	12	$1\frac{27}{64}$		$1\frac{1}{4}$	7	$1\frac{7}{64}$
				$1\frac{1}{2}$	6	$1\frac{11}{32}$

Decimal Equivalent Size of the Number Drills

Drill No.	Decimal Equivalent	Drill No.	Decimal Equivalent	Drill No.	Decimal Equivalent
80	.0135	53	.0595	26	.1470
79	.0145	52	.0635	25	.1495
78	.0160	51	.0670	24	.1520
77	.0180	50	.0700	23	.1540
76	.0200	49	.0730	22	.1570
75	.0210	48	.0760	21	.1590
74	.0225	47	.0785	20	.1610
73	.0240	46	.0810	19	.1660
72	.0250	45	.0820	18	.1695
71	.0260	44	.0860	17	.1730
70	.0280	43	.0890	16	.1770
69	.0292	42	.0935	15	.1800
68	.0310	41	.0960	14	.1820
67	.0320	40	.0980	13	.1850
66	.0330	39	.0995	12	.1890
65	.0350	38	.1015	11	.1910
64	.0360	37	.1040	10	.1935
63	.0370	36	.1065	9	.1960
62	.0380	35	.1100	8	.1990
61	.0390	34	.1110	7	.2010
60	.0400	33	.1130	6	.2040
59	.0410	32	.1160	5	.2055
58	.0420	31	.1200	4	.2090
57	.0430	30	.1285	3	.2130
56	.0465	29	.1360	2	.2210
55	.0520	28	.1405	1	.2280
54	.0550	27	.1440		

Decimal Equivalent Size of the Letter Drills

Letter Drill	Decimal Equivalent	Letter Drill	Decimal Equivalent	Letter Drill	Decimal Equivalent
A	.234	J	.277	S	.348
B	.238	K	.281	T	.358
C	.242	L	.290	U	.368
D	.246	M	.295	V	.377
E	.250	N	.302	W	.386
F	.257	O	.316	X	.397
G	.261	P	.323	Y	.404
H	.266	Q	.332	Z	.413
I	.272	R	.339		

ANTI-FREEZE CHART

Temperatures Shown in Degrees Fahrenheit
+32 is Freezing

Cooling System Capacity Quarts	Quarts of **ETHYLENE GLYCOL** Needed for Protection to Temperatures Shown Below													
	1	2	3	4	5	6	7	8	9	10	11	12	13	14
10	+24°	+16°	+ 4°	−12°	−34°	−62°								
11	+25	+18	+ 8	− 6	−23	−47								
12	+26	+19	+10	0	−15	−34	−57°							
13	+27	+21	+13	+ 3	− 9	−25	−45							
14			+15	+ 6	− 5	−18	−34							
15			+16	+ 8	0	−12	−26							
16			+17	+10	+ 2	− 8	−19	−34	−52°					
17			+18	+12	+ 5	− 4	−14	−27	−42					
18			+19	+14	+ 7	0	−10	−21	−34	−50°				
19			+20	+15	+ 9	+ 2	− 7	−16	−28	−42				
20				+16	+10	+ 4	− 3	−12	−22	−34	−48°			
21				+17	+12	+ 6	0	− 9	−17	−28	−41			
22				+18	+13	+ 8	+ 2	− 6	−14	−23	−34	−47°		
23				+19	+14	+ 9	+ 4	− 3	−10	−19	−29	−40		
24				+19	+15	+10	+ 5	0	− 8	−15	−23	−34	−46°	
25				+20	+16	+12	+ 7	+ 1	− 5	−12	−20	−29	−40	−50°
26					+17	+13	+ 8	+ 3	− 3	− 9	−16	−25	−34	−44
27					+18	+14	+ 9	+ 5	− 1	− 7	−13	−21	−29	−39
28					+18	+15	+10	+ 6	+ 1	− 5	−11	−18	−25	−34
29					+19	+16	+12	+ 7	+ 2	− 3	− 8	−15	−22	−29
30					+20	+17	+13	+ 8	+ 4	− 1	− 6	−12	−18	−25

For capacities over 30 quarts divide true capacity by 3. Find quarts Anti-Freeze for the ⅓ and multiply by 3 for quarts to add.

For capacities under 10 quarts multiply true capacity by 3. Find quarts Anti-Freeze for the tripled volume and divide by 3 for quarts to add.

To Increase the Freezing Protection of Anti-Freeze Solutions Already Installed

Cooling System Capacity Quarts	Number of Quarts of **ETHYLENE GLYCOL** Anti-Freeze Required to Increase Protection													
	From +20°F. to					From +10°F. to					From 0°F. to			
	0°	−10°	−20°	−30°	−40°	0°	−10°	−20°	−30°	−40°	−10°	−20°	−30°	−40°
10	1¾	2¼	3	3½	3¾	¾	1½	2¼	2¾	3¼	¾	1½	2	2½
12	2	2¾	3½	4	4½	1	1¾	2½	3¼	3¾	1	1¾	2½	3¼
14	2¼	3¼	4	4¾	5½	1¼	2	3	3¾	4½	1	2	3	3½
16	2½	3½	4½	5¼	6	1¼	2½	3½	4¼	5¼	1¼	2¼	3¼	4
18	3	4	5	6	7	1½	2¾	4	5	5¾	1½	2½	3¾	4¾
20	3¼	4½	5¾	6¾	7½	1¾	3	4¼	5½	6½	1½	2¾	4¼	5¼
22	3½	5	6¼	7¼	8¼	1¾	3¼	4¾	6	7¼	1¾	3¼	4½	5½
24	4	5½	7	8	9	2	3½	5	6½	7½	1¾	3½	5	6
26	4¼	6	7½	8¾	10	2	4	5½	7	8¼	2	3¾	5½	6¾
28	4½	6¼	8	9½	10½	2¼	4¼	6	7½	9	2	4	5¾	7¼
30	5	6¾	8½	10	11½	2½	4½	6½	8	9½	2¼	4¼	6¼	7¾

Test radiator solution with proper hydrometer. Determine from the table the number of quarts of solution to be drawn off from a full cooling system and replace with undiluted anti-freeze, to give the desired increased protection. For example, to increase protection of a 22-quart cooling system containing Ethylene Glycol (permanent type) anti-freeze, from +20°F. to −20°F. will require the replacement of 6¼ quarts of solution with undiluted anti-freeze.

Clubs

Owner's clubs can provide a helpful source of information for you concerning your Fox. Service tips, aftermarket accessories, and other items are often more readily accessible to club members than to the general public. The following is not meant to be an endorsement or a complete listing of all the clubs open to Fox owners, but is given for informational purposes only.

Dasher Owners of America
22 Greene St.
Cumberland, Maryland 21502

This club is open to owners of the following cars: Fox, Dasher, Scirocco, and Rabbit.